The
SUMPHONIA
HYMN SUPPLEMENT

Produced by Sumphonia

Published by Guardian of Truth Foundation

PHRASED NOTATION

ISBN-10: 1-58427-201-5
ISBN-13: 978-158427-2014

Library of Congress Control Number: 2007903112

Guardian of Truth Foundation
P. O. Box 9670
Bowling Green, Kentucky 42102 USA
1-800-428-0121
www.truthbooks.net

Sumphonia
46531 Sundance Trail
Parker, Colorado 80138 USA
www.sumphonia.com

Printed in the United States of America

The *Sumphonia Hymn Supplement* contains 78 psalms, hymns, and spiritual songs of various genre. In one way, the *Sumphonia Hymn Supplement* functions like any other supplement, complementing the repertoire provided by a standard hymnal. In another way, it serves a unique purpose. The *Sumphonia Hymn Supplement* is a prototype, permitting the testing of new features under consideration for a hymnal currently in production.

Of the features to be tested in this supplement, the most novel is a layout scheme we call *phrased notation*. Phrased notation is designed to highlight the content and expression of each hymn. It recognizes and retains literary phrasing and meter, thereby preventing the linear interruption of thoughts that occurs when a couplet or verse is converted from poetic form to paragraph form. Phrased notation is accomplished by wrapping the hymn tune around the hymn. This process and the ensuing notation contrast with the standard notation established in the 1800s when hymn texts were first inserted into musical staves. Phrased notation effectively presents the individual thoughts and overall message of a hymn, thereby enhancing worship.

Another feature, the Metrical Index of Hymns and Tunes, is based on a meter being defined as syllables per line. This simplified definition does not take into account the role of rhyming or the concept of metrical feet, since these aspects of meter are more academic than practical for our purposes. The index groups hymns by meter then couples the tune name to the hymn title. The result is a user-friendly index that will assist worship leaders who wish to interchange hymns and tunes in preparing worship services.

A third feature is suggested arrangements. These arrangements include intuitive harmony for some tunes, scripture readings that can be integrated into hymns, alternating part singing for certain hymns, and optional verses that can be added to specific hymns.

By circulation of this prototype, we are inviting input from the brotherhood at large. Send all comments to info@sumphonia.com. We are also acknowledging those who have helped us in production, including Richard Morrison for the use of his shaped note font, Andrew Couchman for digital notation, Mark Beall for cover design, and the Guardian of Truth Foundation for supporting this project. We are grateful to R. J. Stevens, who taught us much about worship through hymns, and to the hymn writers and music composers who allowed us to publish their hymns.

EDITORS

David Maravilla	Mark Coulson	Charlotte Couchman	Craig Roberts
Steve Wolfgang			

TECHNICAL EDITORS

Sarah Fuhrman	Vicki Dooman	Matthew Bassford	Charles Willis
Mark Bingham	Jennifer King	Glenn Meyer	
Tom Couchman	Ed Holder	Jason Hardin	

ASSOCIATE EDITORS

Don Alexander	Katy Coulson	Frank Himmel	John Trimble
Jeremy Boyd	Jonathan Ellis	Bruce Key	Wayne Walker
Lynette Brown	Laura Greiving	Carl Main	Howard Whittlesey
Scott Brown	Bill Hall	Keith Roland	Aleisha Zavala
Jennifer Coulson	Matt Harber	Steve Smith	Stanley Zavala

I Sing the Mighty Power of God

1. I sing the might-y pow'r of God That made the moun-tains rise,
2. I sing the good-ness of the Lord, Who filled the earth with food,
3. There's not a plant or flow'r be-low But makes Thy glo-ries known,

That spread the flow-ing seas a-broad And built the loft-y skies.
Who formed the crea-tures through His Word And then pro-nounced them good.
And clouds a-rise and tem-pests blow By or-der from Thy throne;

I sing the wis-dom that or-dained The sun to rule the day;
Lord, how Thy won-ders are dis-played Wher-e'er I turn my eye,
While all that bor-rows life from Thee Is ev-er in Thy care;

The moon shines full at His com-mand, And all the stars o-bey.
If I sur-vey the ground I tread Or gaze up-on the sky.
And eve-ry-where that man can be Thou, God, art pres-ent there.

Hymn: CMD, Isaac Watts
Tune: ELLACOMBE, William H. Monk

B♭ - 4 - SOL

Lamb of God

1. Your on-ly Son, no sin to hide, But You have sent Him from Your side
   Your gift of love they cru-ci-fied, They laughed and scorned Him as He died;
2. I was so lost I should have died, But You have brought me to Your side

To walk up-on this guilt-y sod And to be-come the Lamb of God.)
The hum-ble king they named a fraud And sac-ri-ficed the Lamb of God.)
To be led by Your staff and rod, And to be called a lamb of God.

CHORUS

O Lamb of God, sweet Lamb of God, I love the ho-ly Lamb of God.

O wash me in His pre-cious blood, My Je-sus Christ, the Lamb of God.

Hymn: LM with chorus, Twila Paris
Tune: Twila Paris
© 1985 StraightWay Music

D - 3 - DO

Hear Me When I Call

3

1. Hear me when I call, O God, my right-eous-ness;
2. Hear my cry, O God, at-tend un-to my prayer,
3. Hear my voice, O God, and cleanse my soul with-in,
4. Hear my prayer, O God, I need Thy cleans-ing power,

Un-to Thee I come in weak-ness and dis-tress.
More and more I need Thy mer-cy and Thy care;
Mer-cy do I need for all my doubts and sin;
Let me feel Thee near each mo-ment of each hour;

Hold my trem-bling hand, lest help-less I should fall;
Clouds of doubt a-rise, and faith grows weak and small,
On-ly in Thy grace I trust my all in all,
Hold my trem-bling hand, lest help-less I should fall,

O hear me, Lord, hear me, O hear me when I call!
O hear me, Lord, hear me, O hear me when I call!
O hear me, Lord, hear me, O hear me when I call!
O hear me, Lord, hear me, O hear me when I call!

Hymn: 11.11.11.12., Tillit S. Teddlie
Tune: Tillit S. Teddlie
© 1962 Tillit S. Teddlie

B♭ - 3 - SOL

Glory Yet Untold

4

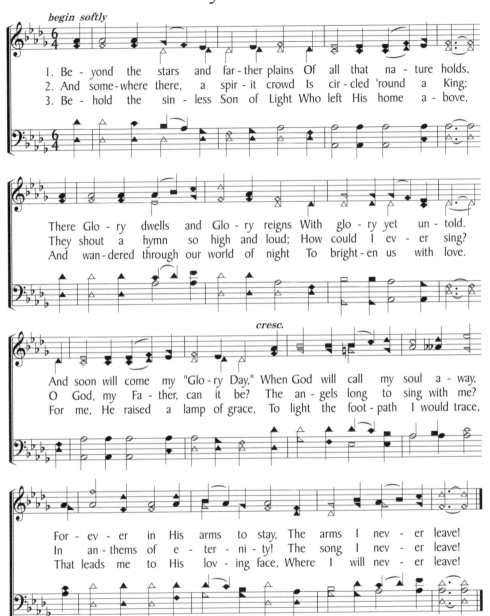

begin softly

1. Be - yond the stars and far - ther plains Of all that na - ture holds,
2. And some - where there, a spir - it crowd Is cir - cled 'round a King;
3. Be - hold the sin - less Son of Light Who left His home a - bove,

There Glo - ry dwells and Glo - ry reigns With glo - ry yet un - told.
They shout a hymn so high and loud; How could I ev - er sing?
And wan - dered through our world of night To bright - en us with love.

cresc.

And soon will come my "Glo - ry Day," When God will call my soul a - way,
O God, my Fa - ther, can it be? The an - gels long to sing with me?
For me, He raised a lamp of grace, To light the foot - path I would trace,

For - ev - er in His arms to stay, The arms I nev - er leave!
In an - thems of e - ter - ni - ty! The song I nev - er leave!
That leads me to His lov - ing face, Where I will nev - er leave!

Hymn: 8.6.8.6.8.8.8.8.6., Kelly R. Hersey and C. A. R.
Tune: Kelly R. Hersey
© 1995 Jo L. Hersey

D♭ - 2 - SOL

Evensong

5

1. The eve - ning light is fail - ing, The sun has passed a - way;
2. In peace be - yond all sor - row, We let our eye - lids close,
p 3. Our God, as we a - dore You, We learn that life shall pass;

Our Fa - ther's hand is veil - ing The splen - dor of the day,
Un - wor - ried by to - mor - row, Un - trou - bled by our foes.
All flesh is dust be - fore You, Its glo - ry, like the grass.

But still we know His fa - vor And see it shine more bright
Our Shep - herd will not fail us; He watch - es for His sheep;
But You will not for - sake us, Nor leave Your word un - done;

In Je - sus Christ our Sav - ior, Our pure and change - less Light.
No e - vil will as - sail us, For He will nev - er sleep.
mf From dark - ness You will wake us To glo - ry like the sun.

Hymn: 7.6.7.6.D, M. W. Bassford
Tune: EVENSONG, Matthew L. Harber
© 2005 M. W. Bassford and Matthew L. Harber

A♭ - 3 - DO

6   Still the Cause Before Us

1. Let all who stand with Christ the Lord, Each good and faith-ful ser-vant,
2. The ear-ly saints held fast in-deed, And One would soon re-ward them;
3. Al-might-y God, whose out-stretched arm Is cer-tain to de-fend us,
p 4. O God, we know by press-ing on, A field is ev-er near-ing;

Take up the shield and bear the sword, With heart and spir-it fer-vent.
For mount-ed on His bat-tle steed, "The Word of God" came toward them.
We pray wher-e'er the pres-ent harm, "In-to the con-flict, send us!"
Where all our mor-tal strength is gone, We lie down in the clear-ing.

Be-hind the Rock of Ag-es, And armed with ho-ly pag-es,
And through the slaugh-ter glo-rious, His ar-my rode vic-to-rious!
By call-ing and e-lec-tion, With pow-er and pro-tec-tion,
Should night-fall o-ver-take us, *f* The morn-ing hymn will wake us!

rit.

If God be for us, who can fear? O let us be cou-ra-geous!
Their cause, now aged two thou-sand years, Is still the cause be-fore us.
Our cross of du-ty leads from here To crowns of res-ur-rec-tion.
And when our Life and Light ap-pears, Im-mor-tal Fa-ther, take us.

Hymn: 8.7.8.7.7.7.8.7., C. A. R.
Tune: EAKIN, based on Robert Schumann; arr. C. A. R. and Sarah J. Roberts
© 2002 M. W. Bassford

G - 2 - DO

You Are My Strength

7

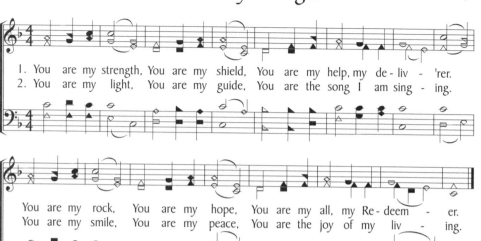

1. You are my strength, You are my shield, You are my help, my de-liv-'rer.
2. You are my light, You are my guide, You are the song I am sing-ing.

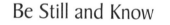

You are my rock, You are my hope, You are my all, my Re-deem-er.
You are my smile, You are my peace, You are the joy of my liv-ing.

Hymn: LM, Glenda B. Schales
Tune: Glenda B. Schales
© 1999 Glenda B. Schales

F - 4 - MI

Be Still and Know

8

1. Be still and know that I am God. Be still and know that I am God.
2. I am the Lord Who strength-ens you. I am the Lord Who strength-ens you.

Be still and know that I am God.
I am the Lord Who strength-ens you.

Hymn: 8.8.8., Anonymous
Tune: Anonymous

D - 3 - SOL

The Spacious Firmament

1. The spa - cious fir - ma - ment on high,
2. Soon as the eve - ning shades pre - vail,
3. What tho' in sol - emn si - lence all

With all the blue e - the - real sky,
The moon takes up the won - drous tale,
Move round this dark ter - res - trial ball?

And span - gled heav'ns, a shin - ing frame,
And night - ly to the lis - t'ning earth
What tho' no re - al voice nor sound

Their great O - rig - i - nal pro - claim.
Re - peats the sto - ry of her birth;
A - mid the rad - iant orbs be found?

Th'un - wear - ied sun, from day to day,
While all the stars that round her burn
In rea - son's ear they all re - joice,

Does his Cre - a - tor's pow'r dis - play
And all the plan - ets in their turn
And ut - ter forth a glo - rious voice,

And pub - lish - es to eve - ry land
Con - firm the tid - ings as they roll
For - ev - er sing - ing as they shine,

The work of an al - might - y hand.
And spread the truth from pole to pole.
"The hand that made us is di - vine."

Hymn: LMD, Joseph Addison
Tune: CREATION, Franz J. Haydn

Bb - 2 - SOL

10 Guide Me, O Thou Great Jehovah

1. Guide me, O Thou great Je - ho - vah, Pil - grim through this bar - ren land;
2. O - pen now the crys - tal foun - tain, Whence the heal - ing wa - ters flow;
3. When I tread the verge of Jor - dan, Bid my anx - ious fears sub - side;

I am weak, but Thou art might - y, Hold me with Thy pow'r - ful hand;
Let the fire and cloud - y pil - lar Lead me all my jour - ney through;
Bear me through the swell - ing cur - rent, Land me safe on Ca - naan's side;

Bread of heav - en, Bread of heav - en, Feed me till I want no more.
Strong De - liv - 'rer, Strong De - liv - 'rer, Be Thou still my strength and shield,
Songs of prais - es, Songs of prais - es I will ev - er give to Thee,

Feed me till I want no more.
Be Thou still my strength and shield.
I will ev - er give to Thee.

Hymn: 8.7.8.7.8.7., William Williams; tr: vs. 1 Peter Williams, vv. 2-3 William Williams
Tune: CWM RHONDDA, John Hughes

G - 4 - SOL

The Rock of My Heart

1. My Lord, I need noth-ing be-side You; With-out You, I could not have stood.
2. When I was dis-tressed and em-bit-tered, By things I could not un-der-stand,
3. I know that Your coun-sel will guide me In wis-dom, de-vo-tion, and love,

Your prom-ise is my hope and my ref-uge; Your near-ness, my strength and my good.
Your pres-ence was con-tin-ual-ly with me; You al-ways took hold of my hand.
And af-ter-ward You'll call me to glo-ry To dwell in Your pres-ence a-bove.

CHORUS

My heart may be bro-ken with-in me; My earth-ly strength may de-part.

But You are my por-tion for-ev-er, You are the Rock of my heart.

rit.

You are the Rock of my heart.

Hymn: Irr., M. W. Bassford, from Psalm 73
Tune: Glenda B. Schales
© 2000 Lynn and Janet Wall

F - 3 - MI

Thy Word

Thy Word is a lamp un-to my feet and a light un-to my path.

Thy Word is a lamp un-to my feet and a light un-to my path.

When I feel a-fraid, Think I've lost my way, Still You're there right be-side me.

Noth-ing will I fear As long as You are near; Please be near me to the end.

Thy Word is a lamp un-to my feet and a light un-to my path.

Thy Word is a lamp un-to my feet and a light un-to my path.

You're the light un-to my path.

Hymn: Irr., Amy Grant and Michael W. Smith
Tune: Michael W. Smith and Amy Grant
© 1984 Bug and Bear Music/Meadowgreen Music Co.

F - 4 - DO

The Feast of Love 13

1. Sav - ior, as we eat Your sup-per, We are joined with those a - part,
2. Ho - ly ones through-out the ag - es Al - so join us as we sup;
3. All Your church is one in wor-ship, One in heart with You a - bove,

Joined in mem - o - ry and wor - ship, Near in wor - thi - ness of heart.
Saints u - nit - ed, past and fu - ture, Shar - ers in the bread and cup.
Tast - ing one e - ter - nal shar - ing As we keep the feast of love.

Hymn: 8.7.8.7., M. W. Bassford
Tune: C. E. Couchman
© 2001 M. W. Bassford and C. E. Couchman

F - 4 - DO

Be Strong and Courageous

1. Be strong and cou-ra-geous, you hosts of the Lord!
2. Be strong and cou-ra-geous; through God you will win,
3. Be strong and cou-ra-geous; con-sid-er His law;

Rise up for the bat-tle and gird on your swords!
Though great be the ar-mies of er-ror and sin.
Re-gard it with rev-'rence; per-form it with awe.

The land of His prom-ise is yours now by right;
Your Cap-tain will lead you to con-quer the land;
Be care-ful to fol-low all God has de-creed,

Take all He has giv-en; go forth to the fight!
His arm can-not fail you, and they can-not stand.
For then He will bless you, and you will suc-ceed.

Hymn: 11.11.11.11. with chorus, M. W. Bassford
Tune: Glenda B. Schales
© 2001 Glenda B. Schales

Eb - 3 - DO

Step by Step

O God, You are my God, and I will ev - er praise You.

I will seek You in the morn - ing, And I will learn to walk in Your ways,

And step by step You'll lead me, And I will fol-low You all of my days.

days. And I will fol-low You all of my days,

And I will fol - low You all of my days,

And step by step You'll lead me, And I will fol-low You all of my days.

Hymn: Irr., David (Beaker) Strasser
Tune: David (Beaker) Strasser; arr. Ken Young
© 1991 BMG Songs, Inc. (ASCAP) / Kid Brothers of St. Frank Publishing (ASCAP).
All rights on behalf of Kid Brothers of St. Frank Publishing administered by BMG Songs, Inc.

Ab - 4 - SOL

Father, Help Us Raise Our Children 16

1. Lit - tle chil - dren, from a - bove, Sent to us with joy and love,
2. O how ten - der is the sight: Lit - tle ones in bed at night,
3. Lit - tle chil - dren soon are grown; Can they face the world a - lone?
p 4. When our time to go draws near, We may leave our chil - dren here;

Bring a hope so clear and bright, Fa - ther, help us raise them right.
Par - ents pray - ing at their feet, "Fa - ther, keep them pure and sweet."
As they strive and strug - gle through, Fa - ther, let them turn to You.
To the new land, far a - way, Fa - ther, bring them home some day.

Hymn: 7.7.7.7., C. A. R.
Tune: COLUMBIA, C. A. R.
© 1995 David and Nelline Watts

G - 3 - MI

17   My Faith Has Found a Resting Place

1. My faith has found a rest - ing place, Not in a man - made creed:
2. E - nough for me that Je - sus saves; This ends my fear and doubt.
3. My soul is rest - ing on the Word, The liv - ing Word of God,
4. The great Phy - si - cian heals the sick; The lost He came to save.

I trust the ev - er liv - ing One, That He for me will plead.
A sin - ful soul I come to Him, He will not cast me out.
Sal - va - tion in my Sav - ior's name, Sal - va - tion through His blood.
For me His pre - cious blood He shed, For me His life He gave.

CHORUS

I need no oth - er ar - gu - ment, I need no oth - er plea;

It is e - nough that Je - sus died And rose a - gain for me.

Hymn: CM with chorus, Eliza E. Hewitt
Tune: LANDÅS, André E. M. Grétry; arr. William J. Kirkpatrick

G - 3 - SOL

Let the Whole Creation Cry

1. Let the whole cre - a - tion cry: "Al - le - lu - ia!"
2. Praise Him, all ye hosts a - bove, Al - le - lu - ia!
3. Men and wo - men, young and old, Al - le - lu - ia!

Glo - ry to the Lord on high! Al - le - lu - ia!
Ev - er bright and fair in love, Al - le - lu - ia!
Raise the an - them man - i - fold, Al - le - lu - ia!

Heav'n and earth, a - wake and sing: "Al - le - lu - ia!"
Sun and moon, lift up your voice! Al - le - lu - ia!
Chil - dren with your hap - py hearts, Al - le - lu - ia!

God is good and God is King! Al - le - lu - ia!
Night and stars, in God re - joice! Al - le - lu - ia!
In this wor - ship sing your parts, Al - le - lu - ia!

Hymn: 7.7.7.7. with alleluias, Stopford A. Brooke
Tune: LLANFAIR, Robert Williams; arr. John Roberts and C. A. R.

E - 4 - DO

19   Living Water, Bread of Life

1. God sends springs in - to the val - leys, Flow - ing soft - ly through the hills.
2. God makes seed we plant for har - vest, Grows the seed - ling in the field,
3. God pro - vides in great a - bun - dance; Of His boun - ty He has said:

God sends streams down from the moun - tains, Leap - ing o - ver rocks and rills.
Rip - ens grain for us to ga - ther, For the good bread it will yield.
"I'll not see the saints for - sak - en Or the right - eous beg - ging bread."

He fills riv - ers; He fills o - ceans. Oh! What boun - ty o - ver - flows!
He made man - na sent from heav - en. Oh! What boun - ty He be - stows!
Fa - ther, keep it still be - fore me: Great - est boun - ty You be - stow

rit.

But His gift of Liv - ing Wa - ter Quench - es thirst with - in my soul.
Yet the Bread of Life He gives me Feeds the hun - ger of my soul.
Is the Christ, the Liv - ing Wa - ter, Bread of Life to fill my soul.

Hymn: 8.7.8.7.D, Gayle D. Garrison
Tune: Gayle D. Garrison; arr. R. J. Stevens
© 1999 Gayle D. Garrison

A♭ - 4 - DO

My Faith, It Is an Oaken Staff

1. My faith, it is an oak-en staff, A trav-'ler's well-loved aid.
2. I have a guide, and in His steps When trav-el-ers have trod,
3. My faith, it is an oak-en staff; O let me on it lean!

My faith, it is a weap-on stout, A sol-dier's trust-y blade.
Wheth-er be-neath was flint-y rock Or yield-ing grass-y sod,
My faith, it is a trust-y sword; May false-hood find it keen!

I'll trav-el on and still be stirred By si-lent thought or so-cial word,
They cared not, but with force un-spent, Un-moved by pain, they on-ward went,
Thy spir-it, Lord, to me im-part; O make me what Thou ev-er art,

By all my per-ils un-de-terred, A sol-dier-pil-grim staid.
Un-stayed by pleas-ures, still they bent Their zeal-ous course to God.
Of pa-tient and cou-ra-geous heart, As all true saints have been.

Hymn: 8.6.8.6.8.8.8.6., Thomas Lynch
Tune: THE STAFF OF FAITH; arr. alt. C. A. R.

E - 4 - SOL

May This My Glory Be

21

1. Je - sus, and shall it ev - er be, A mor - tal man a - shamed of Thee?
2. A - shamed of Je - sus! soon - er far Let eve - ning blush to own a star;
3. A - shamed of Je - sus! yes, I may, When I've no guilt to wash a - way;
4. Till then, nor is my boast-ing vain, Till then I boast a sav - ior slain;

A - shamed of Thee, Whom an - gels praise, Whose glo - ries shine through end - less days?
He sheds the beams of light di - vine O'er this be - night - ed soul of mine.
No tears to wipe, no good to crave, No fears to quell, no soul to save.
And O, may this my glo - ry be, That Christ is not a - shamed of me.

CHORUS

And O, may this my glo - ry be, My glo - ry be, my glo - ry be,

That Christ is not a - shamed of me, Is not a - shamed of me.

Hymn: LM with chorus, Joseph Grigg; chorus arr. Tillit S. Teddlie
Tune: Tillit S. Teddlie
© 1972 Tillit S. Teddlie

C - 2 - MI

I Will Wake the Dawn with Praises

1. Dawn and sun-set, fierce and joy-ful, Each re-flect His might-y ways.
2. Stars will joy in prais-es from me; "Less-er light" will know my voice.
3. Shout His glo-ry, broth-ers, sis-ters; Laud His name and do His will.

With the sea and sky be-fore me, I will give Him all my praise.
When I give my God His glo-ry, Night will hear me and re-joice.
Like the sands up-on the shore-line Are the prais-es due Him still.

CHORUS

I will wake the dawn with prais-es! I will speak His name a-broad.
I will sure-ly wake the dawn with prais-es! I will sure-ly speak His name a-broad.

I will wor-ship Him for-ev-er, He my Lord, my on-ly God.

Hymn: 8.7.8.7. with chorus, Sarah J. Fuhrman
Tune: Glenda B. Schales
© 2001 Sarah J. Fuhrman and Glenda B. Schales

Ab - 4 -SOL

Our Faithful Care

1. "Glo - ry to God!" In all lam - en - ta - tion,
2. "Glo - ry to God!" In all trib - u - la - tion,
3. "Glo - ry to God!" In all our to - mor - rows,

Teach us to suf - fer like our Lord;
Meas - ure the por - tion each can bear;
Read - y Thy throne for com - ing prayers,

Then may we seek Thy ho - ly com - pas - sion,
Cov - er new pain with fresh con - so - la - tion—
Some fu - ture tears, or some dis - tant sor - rows;

Our arms out - stretched, Thy love out - poured.
Balm for our hearts to heal and share.
Be Thou our God, our Faith - ful Care.

Hymn: 10.8.10.8., C. A. R. and Glenda B. Schales
Tune: PARAKALEO, Glenda B. Schales and C. A. R.
© 1997 Benjamin and Adele Holt

G - 4 - SOL

Shall We Gather at the River?

1. Shall we gath-er at the riv-er, Where bright an-gel feet have trod,
2. On the mar-gin of the riv-er, Wash-ing up its sil-ver spray,
3. Ere we reach the shin-ing riv-er, Lay we eve-ry bur-den down;
4. At the smil-ing of the riv-er, Mir-ror of the Sav-ior's face,
5. Soon we'll reach the sil-ver riv-er, Soon our pil-grim-age will cease;

With its crys-tal tide for-ev-er Flow-ing by the throne of God?
We will talk and wor-ship ev-er, All the hap-py gold-en day.
Grace our spir-its will de-liv-er, And pro-vide a robe and crown.
Saints, whom death will nev-er sev-er, Lift their songs of sav-ing grace.
Soon our hap-py hearts will quiv-er With the mel-o-dy of peace.

CHORUS

Yes, we'll gath-er at the riv-er, The beau-ti-ful, the beau-ti-ful riv-er;

Gath-er with the saints at the riv-er That flows by the throne of God.

Hymn: 8.7.8.7. with chorus, Robert Lowry
Tune: Robert Lowry

E♭ - 4 - MI

25　Savior and Friend

1. Rest of the wea - ry, Joy of the sad,
2. Wealth of the giv - ing, Heart of the kind,
3. Song of the sigh - ing, Lamp of the led,

Hope of the drear - y, Light of the glad;
Breath of the liv - ing, Sight of the blind;
Prayer of the dy - ing, Life of the dead;

Ref - uge from dan - ger, Strength to the end,
Path of the low - ly, Crown at the end,
Be my En - deav - or, Un - to the end,

Home of the stran - ger, Sav - ior and Friend.
Bread of the ho - ly, Sav - ior and Friend.
Love me for - ev - er, Sav - ior and Friend.

Hymn: 5.4.5.4.D, J. S. B. Monsell, M. W. Bassford, C. A. R.
Tune: COULSON, C. A. R.
© 2000 Mark and Sylvia Coulson

G -3 - DO
†

When I Can Read My Title Clear

1. When I can read my ti-tle clear To man-sions in the skies,
2. Should earth a-gainst my soul en-gage And fier-y darts be hurled,
3. Let cares, like wild del-ug-es come, And storms of sor-row fall!
4. There shall I bathe my wea-ry soul In seas of heav'n-ly rest,

I'll bid fare-well to eve-ry fear And wipe my weep-ing eyes,
Then I can smile at Sa-tan's rage And face a frown-ing world,
May I but safe-ly reach my home, My God, my heav'n, my all,
And not a wave of trou-ble roll A-cross my peace-ful breast,

And wipe my weep-ing eyes, And wipe my weep-ing eyes.
And face a frown-ing world, And face a frown-ing world.
My God, my heav'n, my all, My God, my heav'n, my all.
A-cross my peace-ful breast, A-cross my peace-ful breast.

I'll bid fare-well to eve-ry fear And wipe my weep-ing eyes.
Then I can smile at Sa-tan's rage And face a frown-ing world.
May I but safe-ly reach my home, My God, my heav'n, my all.
And not a wave of trou-ble roll A-cross my peace-ful breast.

Hymn: CM, Isaac Watts
Tune: PISGAH, from *Kentucky Harmony*, 1817; arr. alt. C. A. R.

A♭ - 4 - SOL

27 The Army of Our Lord

1. O men of age, O men of youth, Lift up your i - dle swords;
2. Our Lord sees eve - ry Chris - tian die, And feels each dy - ing breath,
3. Our el - ders, long in bat - tle years, A - las, be - gin to fade;
4. Our breth - ren, dead be - neath the plain, Whose spir - its nev - er died,

Come fight with us who fight for truth: The Ar - my of our Lord.
And calls out from a field near - by, "Be faith - ful un - to death."
But from the ranks, young men ap - pear And lead their first cru - sade.
Rise up to march and shout a - gain, "O Christ, be glo - ri - fied!"

CODA

pp "O Christ, be glo - ri - fied!"

Hymn: CM, C. A. R.
Tune: ST. FLAVIAN, from *Day's Psalter*, 1562
© 1994 Richard and Anne Morrison

F - 4 - DO

28 Opening Prayer

1. Lord, as we meet this day, Give us one mind to pray;
2. O may our world - ly cares Give place to thoughts more pure
3. Now in Your pres - ence, Lord, We praise Your ho - ly Word,

O - pen our hearts to say that You are Lord.
And true de - sire to serve You on - ly, Lord.
Who was and is and ev - er shall be Lord. A - men.

Hymn: 6.6.10., C. E. Couchman
Tune: COSTILLA, C. E. Couchman
© 1985 C. E. Couchman

Awesome God 29

Our God is an awe - some God; He reigns from heav - en a - bove

With wis - dom, pow'r and love. Our God is an awe - some God. God.

Our God is an awe - some God. Our God is an awe - some God.

Hymn: 7.7.6.7., Rich Mullins
Tune: Rich Mullins
© 1988 BMG Songs, Inc.

F minor - 2 - LA

30   O Magnify My Master

1. O mag-ni-fy my Mas-ter, Ex-alt His ho-ly name.
2. With words of ad-o-ra-tion, With songs of end-less praise,
3. As well as I may praise Thee In my own frag-ile way;

His name I praise for-ev-er, For-ev-er and a-gain.
From hearts that know but glad-ness, For love of heav-en's ways,
Nor with my soul, O Je-sus, Could I Thy love re-pay.

To heights of all Thy glo-ry, To heights be-yond the sky,
And from yon realms, ma-jes-tic, Where saints of ag-es gone,
I sing of all Thy grac-es, I bow and laud Thy care,

To far be-yond cre-a-tion, To Him let prais-es fly.
With joy my soul would cher-ish, Praise Je-sus all day long.
And take of all Thy bless-ings. I see them ev-ery-where.

Hymn: 7.6.7.6.D, O. E. Landrum
Tune: O. E. Landrum; arr. R. J. Stevens
© 1998 O. E. Landrum and R. J. Stevens

F - 4 - MI

We Praise Thee, O God, Our Redeemer   31

1. We praise Thee, O God, our Re - deem - er, Cre - a - tor;
2. We wor - ship Thee, God of our fa - thers; we bless Thee.
3. With voic - es u - nit - ed our prais - es we of - fer,

In grate - ful de - vo - tion our trib - ute we bring.
Through life's storm and tem - pest our Guide hast Thou been.
And glad - ly our songs of true wor - ship we raise.

We lay it be - fore Thee; we kneel and a - dore Thee.
When per - ils o'er - take us, Thou wilt not for - sake us,
Thy strong arm will guide us; our God is be - fore us.

We bless Thy ho - ly name; glad prais - es we sing.
And with Thy help, O Lord, life's bat - tles we win.
To Thee, our great Re - deem - er, ev - er be praise.

Hymn: 12.11.12.11., Julia B. Cory   D - 3 - SOL
Tune: KREMSER; arr. Eduard Kremser

32 Theophany
(High above the Seraphim)

No staccato

1. High a-bove the ser-a-phim Sounds an ev-er-last-ing hymn;
2. Praise the Seed of A-bra-ham! All do-min-ion to the Lamb!
mp 3. Night to night I come to Him, Kneel be-fore His di-a-dem;

Voic-es ech-o through the hall And shake the tem-ple wall.
Sing of Him, in glo-ry slain, "Lord God Al-might-y reigns!"
While a thou-sand thou-sand sing, I fall be-fore the King.

Liv-ing crea-tures bless the King, Four and twen-ty eld-ers sing,
Shout the God-breathed proph-e-cy: "He Who was will ev-er be!"
Soon will He be chang-ing me: Clothed in im-mor-tal-i-ty,

rit. last verse

"Wor-thy He Who o-ver-came"; "The Word of God" His name.
Kings of earth have passed a-way! The Son is Lord this day!
Swal-lowed up in vic-to-ry, And ev-er-more to be.

Hymn: 7.7.7.6.D, C. A. R.
Tune: MAZURKA, Frederic Chopin; arr. C. A. R.
© 2001 David and Jimona Maravilla

E - 3 - SOL

Servant Song

1. Make me a serv-ant, Just like Your Son,
2. Make me a serv-ant, Take all my pride,
3. Make me a serv-ant, Filled by Your might,

For He was a serv-ant; Please make me one.
For I would be low-ly, Hum-ble in-side;
And may all my la-bors Shine with Your light.

Make me a serv-ant, Do what You must do
Giv-ing to oth-ers With all that I do
Show me Your foot-steps And what I should do;

rit.

To make me a serv-ant; Make me like You.
In love for my broth-er; Make me like You.
For now and for-ev-er, Make me like You.

Hymn: Irr., vs. 1 alt. Tim Jennings, vv. 2-3 M. W. Bassford
Tune: Traditional; arr. Richard L. Morrison
© 2000 Tim Jennings

F - 3 - MI

34   For You Have Promised

1. O Fa-ther, draw me close to You.
2. I lift my hand to reach Your face,
p 3. I speak Your name in-to the night,
4. Se-cure my heart, Lord, as I kneel.

Calm now my spir-it, peace re-new.
Find in Your arms a hid-ing place,
Seek through the pain Your heal-ing light.
Make sure my trust, my all, I yield.

And yes, I know You hear, for You are near,
To be en-fold-ed there with-in Your care,
And then I will not fear, for You are here,
Then I'll be one with You in all I do,

For You have prom-ised, and I be-lieve.

CHORUS

Faster

Then I will praise_____ Your name for - ev - er.
        Then I will praise   I'll praise Your name
        Then I will praise Your name for - ev - er, praise Your name
    Praise   Your   name   for - ev - er,   Then

I'll give You thanks and mag - ni - fy Your lov - ing fa - vor.
        fa - vor for me.

And I will tell_____ of Your sal - va - tion,
        Then I will tell   I'll tell all men
        Then I will tell of Your sal va - tion, tell all men
    Tell   of   Your   sal - va - tion, tell all men,

For all Your prom - is - es are true, and I be - lieve.

Hymn: Irr., Glenda B. Schales
Tune: Glenda B. Schales
© 1996 Glenda B. Schales

E♭ - 4 - DO

35   Loved Ones

1. O Lord, help me main-tain An un-der-stand-ing heart,
2. Lord, help me un-der-stand That loved ones move a-way,
3. Help me re-mem-ber, Lord, When loved ones fall in sin,
4. And Fa-ther, com-fort me When loved ones pass a-way;

So I can o-ver-come the pain When those I love de-part.
But car-ry in-to fu-ture lands Thy word learned yes-ter-day.
With kind-ness they can be re-stored And feel Thy love a-gain.
Re-mind me, Lord, Thy chil-dren see Their love an-oth-er day.

Hymn: SM, C. A. R. Optional vs. 5: John Fawcett
Tune: COLUMBUS, C. A. R.
© 1993 R. J. Stevens

Ab - 3 - SOL

5. When we asunder part,
   It gives us inward pain;
   But we shall still be joined in heart
   And hope to meet again.

36   Come Share the Lord

1. We gath-er here in Je-sus' name;
2. He joins us here, He breaks the bread;
3. We'll gath-er soon where an-gels sing;

His love is burn-ing in our hearts like liv-ing flame,
The Lord Who pours the cup is ris-en from the dead.
We'll see the glo-ry of our Lord and com-ing King.

For through the lov-ing Son the Fa-ther makes us one.
The One we love the most is now our gra-cious Host.
Now we an-tic-i-pate the feast for which we wait.

fine

Come take the bread, come drink the wine, come share the Lord.

1. No one is a strang-er here; Eve-ry one be-longs.
2. We are now a fam-i-ly Of which the Lord is head;

D. C. al fine

Find-ing our for-give-ness here, We in turn for-give all wrongs.
Though un-seen He meets us here In the break-ing of the bread.

Hymn: Irr., Bryan Jeffery Leech
Tune: Bryan Jeffery Leech; arr. Ken Young
© 1984, 1987 Fred Bock Music Company

G - 4 - DO

The Lord Is My Light

1. The Lord is my light and my sal-va-tion. Whom shall I fear?
2. O Lord, lead me now in Thy path straight and e-ven. Teach me Thy way.

And He is my strength, the de-fense of my life. Whom shall I fear?
I will not de-spair; Thy good-ness sus-tains me. Teach me Thy way.

Have mer-cy, O Lord, and an-swer my cry. Turn not a-way.
To dwell in His house all the days of my life: This shall I seek.

For Thou art my help, the God of sal-va-tion. Turn not a-way.
And O to be-hold the Lord in His beau-ty! This shall I seek.

CHORUS

Wait, wait, O wait on the Lord.

Be strong and take cour-age! Wait on the Lord.
Wait, wait on the

Wait, wait, O wait on the Lord.
Lord. _____

rit. last verse

Be strong and take cour-age! Yes, wait on the Lord.

Hymn: Irr., from Psalm 27; arr. C. E. Couchman
Tune: PSALM 27, C. E. Couchman
© 1986 C. E. Couchman

A♭ - 3 - DO

38   The Battle Belongs to the Lord

1. In heav-en-ly ar-mor we'll en-ter the land;
2. When the pow-er of dark-ness comes in like a flood,
3. When your en-e-my press-es in hard, do not fear;

The bat-tle be-longs to the Lord.
The bat-tle be-longs to the Lord.
The bat-tle be-longs to the Lord.

No weap-on that's fash-ioned a-gainst us will stand;
He's raised up a stand-ard, the pow'r of His blood;
Take cour-age, my friend, your re-demp-tion is near;

The bat-tle be-longs to the Lord.
The bat-tle be-longs to the Lord.
The bat-tle be-longs to the Lord.

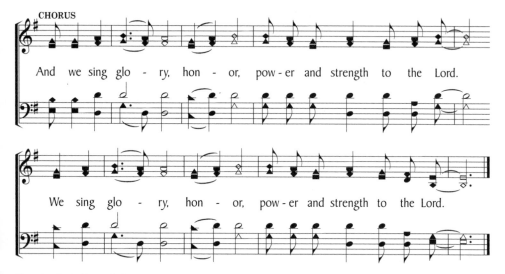

CHORUS

And we sing glo - ry, hon - or, pow - er and strength to the Lord.

We sing glo - ry, hon - or, pow - er and strength to the Lord.

Hymn: Irr., Jamie Owens-Collins
Tune: Jamie Owens-Collins; arr. Reid Lancaster
© 1985 Fairhill Music

E minor - 4 - MI

God of Prayer
39

Gently

1. God al - might - y, God a - round me, Be my Pres - ence eve - ry - where!
2. God all - lov - ing, all - for - giv - ing, Who could know the hours we share?
3. Fa - ther, when You take my spir - it, Grant me strength for one last prayer!

Near - er since the day You found me: God so near! O God of prayer!
End - less plead - ing, full thanks - giv - ing, You and I, so long in prayer!
Faint it be, though, You would hear it; Hear me then! O God, be there!

Hymn: 8.7.8.7., C. A. R.
Tune: Based on DIR, DIR JEHOVAH, C. A. R. and J. A. Freylinghausen
© 1999 Lonnie and Susan Corley

D - 4 - DO

40   I Stand in Awe

You are beau-ti-ful be-yond de-scrip-tion, Too mar-vel-ous for words,

Too won-der-ful for com-pre-hen-sion, Like noth-ing ev-er seen or heard.

Who can grasp Your in-fi-nite wis-dom, Who can fath-om the depth of Your love?

You are beau-ti-ful be-yond de-scrip-tion, Maj-es-ty en-throned a-bove.

CHORUS

And I stand, I stand in awe of You; I stand, I stand in awe of You;

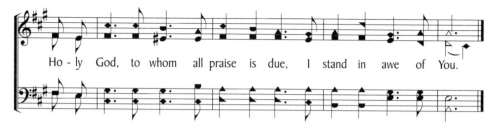

Ho - ly God, to whom all praise is due, I stand in awe of You.

Hymn: Irr., Mark Altrogge
Tune: Mark Altrogge; arr. Reid Lancaster
© 1987 People of Destiny International/Pleasant Hills Music

A - 4 - MI

We Shall Stand Before the Throne 41

1. We shall stand be - fore the throne, Stand with all, but stand a - lone,
2. See the vin - di - cat - ed Son, Hear Him say, "De - part. Well done"—
3. On His left, the doomed im - plore, But are locked be - neath a door.
4. But the faith - ful on His right, Wear - ing crowns and gar - ments white,

Face, at last, the A - ged One. God is ho - ly; bow be - fore Him.
Judg - ment sure for eve - ry - one. Christ is ho - ly; lis - ten to Him.
There they burn for - ev - er - more. God is ho - ly; love and fear Him.
Sing for - ev - er in His sight, "Ho - ly, ho - ly, Thou art ho - ly."

Hymn: 7.7.7.8., C. A. R. Optional vs. 5: Philip P. Bliss
Tune: R. J. Stevens
© 1992 Curt and Debbie Roberts

D minor - 4 - LA

5. When He comes, our glorious King,
All His ransomed home to bring,
Then anew this song we'll sing,
"Alleluia! What a Savior!"

42   Give Thanks to the Lord

Give thanks to the Lord! His lov-ing-kind-ness is ev-er-last-ing!

Hymn: Irr., 2 Chronicles 20:21 (NASB)
Tune: EUCHARISTIA, C. A. R.
© Thanksgiving 2003, Mark and Melanie Bingham

F/F# - 4/2 - SOL

Thy Word Is a Treasure   43

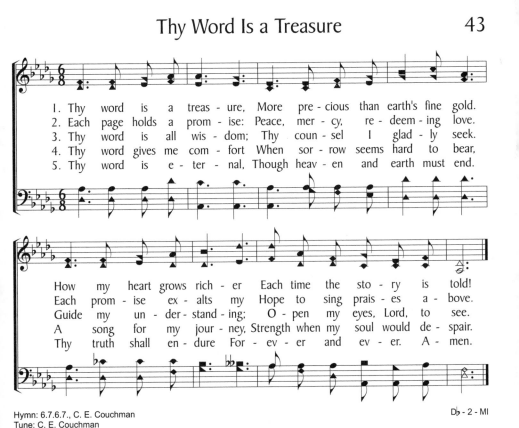

1. Thy word is a treas - ure, More pre - cious than earth's fine gold.
2. Each page holds a prom - ise: Peace, mer - cy, re - deem - ing love.
3. Thy word is all wis - dom; Thy coun - sel I glad - ly seek.
4. Thy word gives me com - fort When sor - row seems hard to bear,
5. Thy word is e - ter - nal, Though heav - en and earth must end.

How my heart grows rich - er Each time the sto - ry is told!
Each prom - ise ex - alts my Hope to sing prais - es a - bove.
Guide my un - der - stand - ing; O - pen my eyes, Lord, to see.
A song for my jour - ney, Strength when my soul would de - spair.
Thy truth shall en - dure For - ev - er and ev - er. A - men.

Hymn: 6.7.6.7., C. E. Couchman
Tune: C. E. Couchman
© 1986 C. E. Couchman

Db - 2 - MI

44   Jesus Is Lord

1. Je-sus is Lord. Wor-thy is the Lamb. Je-sus is God, Ho-ly Great I Am.
2. I lift Him up. Wor-thy is the Lamb. I praise His name, Ho-ly Great I Am.

Je-sus is Prince, on-ly King of kings. Je-sus the Christ, the All of eve-ry-thing.
I crown Him Prince, on-ly King of kings. Je-sus the Christ, my All of eve-ry-thing.

CHORUS

Wor-thy,   wor-thy is the Lamb. Ho-ly,   ho-ly Great I Am.
Wor-thy,   Ho-ly,

On-ly,   on-ly King of kings. Je-sus the Christ, the All of eve-ry-thing.
On-ly,

Hymn: Irr., Gayle D. Garrison
Tune: Gayle D. Garrison; arr. R. J. Stevens
© 2000 Gayle D. Garrison

E - 4 - DO

A Foretaste of Your Rest

1. Gra - cious Fa - ther, Friend di - vine, Con - so - la - tion of the blessed,
2. Should this hour of rest de - part And the joy it brings me cease,
3. Fa - ther, though I can - not see How my path will end be - low,

You have touched this day of mine With a fore - taste of Your rest.
I will bear it in my heart As a prom - ise of Your peace.
Still I know You wait for me Where my heart has longed to go.

Though to - mor - row care may come, Trial a - rise and grief en - sue,
When I strain be - neath new woe Or con - tend with fu - ture sin,
When my bod - y can - not stand, Take my spir - it to Your breast;

rit.

Now I thank You for the time I have spent in joy with You.
From this mo - ment I may know You will bless my life a - gain.
With a fa - ther's gen - tle hands, Bear my soul to Sab - bath rest.

Hymn: 7.7.7.7.D, M. W. Bassford
Tune: COPELAND, Matthew L. Harber
© 2005 M. W. Bassford and Matthew L. Harber

Eb - 3 - MI

46   He's Risen!

1. Night is o - ver; The morn - ing breaks.
2. Night is o - ver; How bright the day!
3. Night is o - ver; Lord, send the day

The sun has ris - en on this first day,
That dares to step in - side the grave
To lift the veil where death once lay.

Just like the morn - ing when Mar - y cried,
And shout to all, "A - wake and see:
Un - seal our hearts; we, too, would sing:

"He's ris - en! I've seen Him! The cru - ci - fied!"
He's ris - en! Christ Je - sus of Cal - va - ry!"
"He's ris - en! My Sav - ior! My Lord! My King!"

Hymn: Irr., C. E. Couchman
Tune: RISEN!, C. E. Couchman
© 1997 C. E. Couchman

D - 3 - MI

In Christ Alone

1. In Christ a-lone my hope is found; He is my light, my strength, my song;
2. In Christ a-lone, Who took on flesh, Full-ness of God in help-less babe!
3. There in the ground His bod-y lay, Light of the world by dark-ness slain;
4. No guilt in life, no fear in death—This is the pow'r of Christ in me;

This cor-ner-stone, this sol-id ground, Firm through the fierc-est drought and storm.
This gift of love and right-eous-ness, Scorned by the ones He came to save.
Then burst-ing forth in glo-rious day, Up from the grave He rose a-gain!
From life's first cry to fi-nal breath, Je-sus com-mands my des-ti-ny.

What heights of love, what depths of peace, When fears are stilled, when striv-ings cease!
Till on that cross as Je-sus died, The wrath of God was sat-is-fied;
And as He stands in vic-to-ry, Sin's curse has lost its grip on me;
No pow'r of hell, no scheme of man Can ev-er pluck me from His hand;

My com-fort-er, my all in all— Here in the love of Christ I stand.
For eve-ry sin on Him was laid— Here in the death of Christ I live.
For I am His and He is mine— Bought with the pre-cious blood of Christ.
Till He re-turns or calls me home— Here in the pow'r of Christ I'll stand.

Hymn: LMD, Keith Getty and Stuart Townend
Tune: Keith Getty and Stuart Townend
© 2001 Kingsway Thankyou Music

Eb - 3 - SOL

48   O How Glorious, Full of Wonder

1. O how glo-rious, full of won-der, Is Thy name o'er all the earth,
2. When we see Thy lights of Heav-en, Moon and stars, Thy pow'r dis-played,
3. Thou hast giv-en man do-min-ion O'er the won-ders of Thy hand,

Thou, Who wrought cre-a-tion's splen-dor, Bring-ing suns and stars to birth!
What is man that Thou shouldst love him, Crea-ture that Thy hand hath made?
Made him fly with ea-gle pin-ion, Mas-ter o-ver sea and land.

Rapt in rev-'rence, we a-dore Thee, Mar-v'ling at Thy mys-tic ways.
Child of earth, yet full of yearn-ing, Mix-ture strange of good and ill,
Soar-ing spire and ru-ined cit-y, These our hopes and fail-ures show.

Hum-bly now, we bow be-fore Thee, Lift-ing up our hearts in praise.
From Thy ways so of-ten turn-ing, Yet Thy love doth seek him still.
Teach us more of hu-man pit-y, That we in Thine im-age grow.

Hymn: 8.7.8.7.D, Curtis Beach
Tune: IN BABILONE, arr. Craig A. Roberts
© 1958 Curtis Beach Estate; arr. © 1998 Craig A. Roberts

A♭ - 4 - DO

Almighty God Beyond the Veil

1. In an-cient times the cho-sen race Pre-pared Je-ho-vah's dwell-ing place.
2. "Be-hold your King!" That shame-ful cry Was ech-oed back as "Cru-ci-fy!"
3. Now we, Je-ho-vah's ran-somed race, May en-ter His Most Ho-ly Place.

The peo-ple feared the voice of Him Who dwelt be-tween the cher-u-bim, the cher-u-bim.
The blood was shed that could a-tone, The Lamb that was Je-ho-vah's own, Je-ho-vah's own.
By faith our prayers as-cend to Him Who reigns a-mong the ser-a-phim, the ser-a-phim.

But once a year their priest would hail Al-might-y God be-yond the veil.
That dark-est hour, His last ex-hale, Ful-filled God's plan and tore the veil.
We bold-ly bow, and thus pre-vail, With God Who dwells be-yond the veil.

CODA

Al-might-y God be-yond the veil.

Hymn: 8.8.8.8.8.8., S. J. Hardin
Tune: C. E. Couchman
© 2003 S. J. Hardin and C. E. Couchman

F minor/A♭ - 4 - MI

50   Lord, Increase My Faith

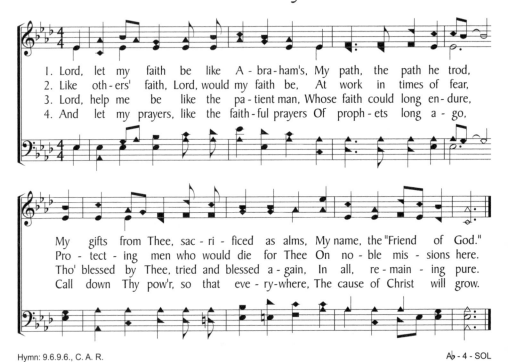

1. Lord, let my faith be like A-bra-ham's, My path, the path he trod,
2. Like oth-ers' faith, Lord, would my faith be, At work in times of fear,
3. Lord, help me be like the pa-tient man, Whose faith could long en-dure,
4. And let my prayers, like the faith-ful prayers Of proph-ets long a-go,

My gifts from Thee, sac-ri-ficed as alms, My name, the "Friend of God."
Pro-tect-ing men who would die for Thee On no-ble mis-sions here.
Tho' blessed by Thee, tried and blessed a-gain, In all, re-main-ing pure.
Call down Thy pow'r, so that eve-ry-where, The cause of Christ will grow.

Hymn: 9.6.9.6., C. A. R.
Tune: R. J. Stevens
© 1994 Jonathan and Barbara Quinn

A♭ - 4 - SOL

51   Nearer, My God, to Thee

1. Near-er, My God, to Thee, Near-er to Thee!
2. Though like the wan-der-er, The sun gone down,
3. There let the way ap-pear, Steps un-to heav'n;
4. Then with my wak-ing thoughts Bright with Thy praise,

E'en though it be a cross That rais - eth me,
Dark - ness be o - ver me, My rest a stone;
All that Thou send - est me In mer - cy giv'n;
Out of my ston - y griefs Beth - el I'll raise;

Still all my song shall be, Near - er, my God, to Thee.
Yet in my dreams I'd be Near - er, my God, to Thee.
An - gels to beck - on me Near - er, my God, to Thee.
So by my woes to be Near - er, my God, to Thee.

Near - er, My God, to Thee, Near - er to Thee!

Hymn: 6.4.6.4.6.6.6.4., vv. 1-5 Sarah F. Adams, vs. 6 Edward H. Bickersteth, Jr.   G - 4 - MI
Tune: BETHANY, Lowell Mason   †

5. Or, if on joyful wing,
 Cleaving the sky,
 Sun, moon and stars forgot,
 Upward I fly;
 Still all my song shall be,
 Nearer, my God, to Thee.
 Nearer, my God, to Thee,
 Nearer to Thee!

6. There in my Father's home,
 Safe and at rest,
 There in my Savior's love,
 Perfectly blest;
 Age after age to be
 Nearer, my God, to Thee.
 Nearer, my God, to Thee,
 Nearer to Thee!

52 Exalted

1. Known be - fore the world; Glimpsed by right-eous men: Son of God.
2. Seen with blind - ed eyes; Met with wick - ed hearts: Son of God.
3. Scorned by those who watched; Loved with - in be - lief: Son of God.

Seen in fu - ture days: the Son of God.
Heard by heed-less ears: the Son of God.
Mocked by all the wise: the Son of God.

Sent as Dav-id's heir; Grant - ed all the earth: Ex - alt - ed.
Wor - shiped with con-tempt; Throned up - on a cross: Ex - alt - ed.
Born to take my death: Je - sus, Son of .... God.

Named an age - less king all the earth Ex - alt - ed.
Crowned with blood and thorns on a cross. Ex - alt - ed.
Slain to give me life: Son of .... God.

Ex - alt - ed. Ex - alt - ed.

Hymn: Irr., M. W. Bassford
Tune: EXALTED, C. E. Couchman
© 1999 C. E. Couchman

G - 4 - DO
...

Hosanna

53

1. Ho - san - na, ho - san - na, Ho - san - na in the high - est;
2. Glo - ry, glo - ry, Glo - ry to the King of kings;

Ho - san - na, ho - san - na, Ho - san - na in the high - est.
Glo - ry, glo - ry, Glo - ry to the King of kings.

CHORUS

Lord, we lift up Your name, With hearts full of praise.
Lord, we lift up Your name, With hearts full, hearts full of praise.

Be ex - alt - ed, O Lord, my God; Ho - san - na in the high - est.
So be ex - alt - ed, O Lord, my God; Ho - san - na in the high - est.

Hymn: Irr., Carl Tuttle
Tune: Carl Tuttle; arr. Reid Lancaster
© 1985 Shadow Spring Music

G - 4 - DO

54   Our Father Forever

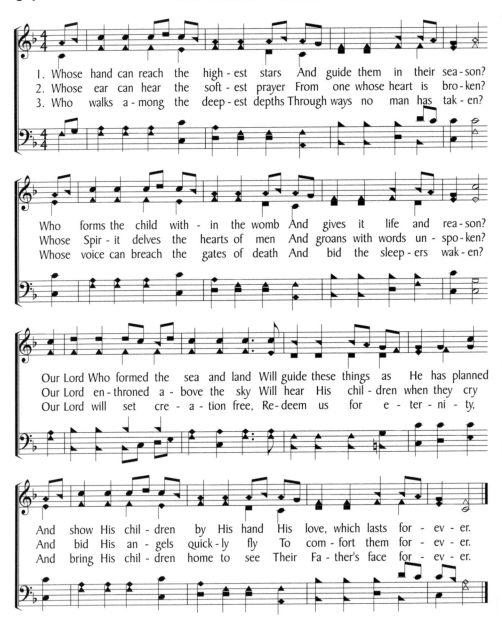

1. Whose hand can reach the high-est stars And guide them in their sea-son?
2. Whose ear can hear the soft-est prayer From one whose heart is bro-ken?
3. Who walks a-mong the deep-est depths Through ways no man has tak-en?

Who forms the child with-in the womb And gives it life and rea-son?
Whose Spir-it delves the hearts of men And groans with words un-spo-ken?
Whose voice can breach the gates of death And bid the sleep-ers wak-en?

Our Lord Who formed the sea and land Will guide these things as He has planned
Our Lord en-throned a-bove the sky Will hear His chil-dren when they cry
Our Lord will set cre-a-tion free, Re-deem us for e-ter-ni-ty,

And show His chil-dren by His hand His love, which lasts for-ev-er.
And bid His an-gels quick-ly fly To com-fort them for-ev-er.
And bring His chil-dren home to see Their Fa-ther's face for-ev-er.

Hymn: 8.7.8.7.8.8.8.7., John D. Trimble
Tune: John D. Trimble; arr. John D. Trimble and Matthew L. Harber
© 2005 John D. Trimble, Matthew L. and Katie Harber

F - 4 - MI

Immanuel, God with Us

1. God in - car - nate, can it be? Pon - der now the mys - ter - y:
2. Shep - herds won - der at the scene: Swad - dling robes for De - i - ty;
3. God Cre - a - tor, now cre - at - ed, Lord of all in in - fan - cy.

He, the Fount of E - ter - nal Life, Must drink the cup of mor - tal - i - ty.
Heav - en's throne now a bed of straw With - in these bor - rowed sta - ble walls.
Hands that light - ed the eve - ning stars Reach out for com - fort in Mar - y's arms.

Im - man - u - el, God with us. Im - man - u - el, God with us.

Our God with us.

Hymn: Irr., C. E. Couchman
Tune: C. E. Couchman
© 1993 C. E. Couchman

A♭ - 4 - DO

56   Soliloquy and Prayer

1. "What shall I say? What shall I say? Fa - ther, save me from this hour?"
2. "I come to Thee. I come to Thee. I am no more in the world."

Men: **All:**

"What shall I say? What shall I say? For this pur-pose, I have come."
"I come to Thee. I come to Thee. Fa - ther, glo - ri - fy Thy Son."

Hymn: 4.4.7.D, arr. C. A. R.
Tune: C. A. R.
© 2002 Thomas and Charlotte Couchman

A - 4 - MI

57   Hide Me, O My Savior, Hide Me

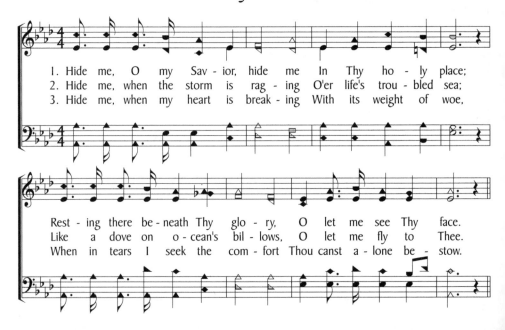

1. Hide me, O my Sav - ior, hide me In Thy ho - ly place;
2. Hide me, when the storm is rag - ing O'er life's trou - bled sea;
3. Hide me, when my heart is break - ing With its weight of woe,

Rest - ing there be - neath Thy glo - ry, O let me see Thy face.
Like a dove on o - cean's bil - lows, O let me fly to Thee.
When in tears I seek the com - fort Thou canst a - lone be - stow.

Hide me, hide me, O bless-ed Sav-ior, hide me;
Hide me, hide me, safe-ly hide me

O Sav-ior, keep me, Safe-ly, O Lord with Thee.
O my Sav-ior, keep Thou me

Hymn: Irr., Fanny J. Crosby
Tune: William H. Doane

Ab - 4 - MI

Purify Us

58

1. Lord, Re-stor-er, Hand un-seen, Come and make Your priest-hood clean;
2. In our weak-ness and de-sire, Melt us with Your cleans-ing fire;
3. To com-plete us, Fa-ther, bless: Make us gifts of right-eous-ness,

Come re-fine our eve-ry part; Pu-ri-fy us, thought and heart.
Burn temp-ta-tion from our minds; Leave Your love and peace be-hind.
Hon-ored in the work we do, Gold-en ves-sels fit for You.

Hymn: 7.7.7.7., M. W. Bassford
Tune: C. E. Couchman
© 2001 M. W. Bassford and C. E. Couchman

A - 4 - MI

I Will Call Upon the Lord

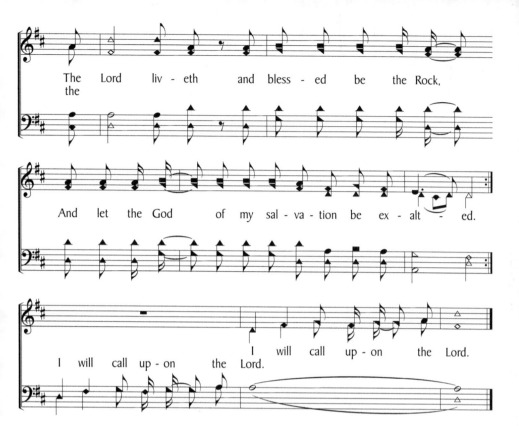

The Lord liv-eth and bless-ed be the Rock, the
And let the God of my sal-va-tion be ex-alt-ed.
I will call up-on the Lord. I will call up-on the Lord.

Hymn: Irr., vs. 1 Michael O'Shields, vv. 2-3 unknown
Tune: Michael O'Shields; arr. Pam Stephenson
© 1981 Sound III, Inc.

D - 4 - DO

2. I will wait upon the Lord;
   He will fill me with new strength.
   I will fly on wings like an eagle.

3. I will look upon the Lord;
   He is all my righteousness.
   He will make His face to shine on me.

60 It Is Time to Build

1. It is time to build in the church of our Lord;
2. Have we built our homes? Have we plant-ed our fields?
3. Let us gath - er wood from the moun-tains of truth;

It is time to con - sid - er our ways.
And for - got - ten the tem - ple of God?
Ham - mer faith, ham - mer hope, ham - mer love.

What a work we share! What a joy to re-peat His prom-ise,
Sound the word to all! Chil-dren, we are His cho-sen rem-nant,
When a soul is saved, What a sight—as Je - ho-vah fills the

giv - en to all who o - bey.
call - ing to peo - ple a - broad.
church with His glo - ry a - bove!

CHORUS

"Now have faith," "Now have cour-age," "Nev - er fear," says our Lord.

"I am with you, My Spir - it a - bides with you."

"Now have faith," "Now have cour-age," "I will fill it with glo - ry."

Build the church! Build the tem - ple of God!

Hymn: Irr., Glenda B. Schales and C. A. R.
Tune: Glenda B. Schales; arr. Glenda B. Schales and C. A. R.
© 1990 Glenda B. Schales

A - 4 - MI

61 O Sons and Daughters, Sing Your Praise

1. O sons and daugh-ters sing your praise, On this most ho-ly day of days,
2. When Mag-da-lene and Sa-lo-me And Ma-ry went where Je-sus lay,
3. An an-gel greet-ed them and said, "The Christ is ris-en from the dead,
4. "How blest are those who do not see, Yet place their faith and trust in Me.

For Christ from death to life is raised!
They found the stone was rolled a-way!
To Gal-i-lee He goes a-head!"
They shall have life e-ter-nal-ly!"

Al - le-lu - ia! Al - le-lu - ia!

Hymn: 8.8.8. with Alleluias, Jean Tisserand; tr. Ruth Duck
Tune: C. A. R.
Tr. © 1993 Pilgrim Press; music © 2006 Craig A. Roberts

G - 4 - SOL

3a. Among disciples Christ appeared;
   "My peace be with you" was His word,
   But Thomas doubted when he heard.
      Alleluia! Alleluia!

3b. "Come, Thomas, see My hands and side;
   I am the one they crucified."
   "My God, my Savior!" Thomas cried.
      Alleluia! Alleluia!

Let Us Know Jehovah

1. Let us know Jehovah; Come, let us press on,
2. Though the Lord has torn us, He will heal a-gain;

For His way is cer-tain, Cer-tain as the dawn.
Though the Lord has struck us, He will bind our pain.

He will come to bless us Like the fall of rain,
Af-ter days of mourn-ing, We will be re-stored,

rit.

Like the rain of spring-time, Wa-ter-ing the plain.
Thus to live be-fore Him; Let us seek the Lord.

Hymn: 6.5.6.5.D, M. W. Bassford
Tune: C. E. Couchman
© 2003 M. W. Bassford and C. E. Couchman

B♭ - 4 - SOL

How Long till the Morning?

1. Con - sid - er the morn - ings of this mor - tal land,
2. up ┊ to the bat - tle, for the skies dawn clear;
3. trum - pet sounds to sig - nal Heav - en's day—

Each a new be - gin - ning from the Mak - er's hand.
Let us gath - er cour - age while the foe draws near.
Res - ur - rec - tion morn - ing when the dead shall wake—

While the storms may gath - er 'gainst the eve - ning sky,
Though the night falls wea - ry, saints of God, march on!
What a glo - rious gath - 'ring when the Lord de - scends

The day breaks cloud - less in the morn - ing.
And He'll raise our ban - ner in the morn - ing.
And we rise to meet Him in the morn - ing.

CHORUS

How long   till we see the morn-ing? How long   till we see Your face?
How   long, my Lord?
How long?   How   long?   O   my Lord

How long,   my Lord, how long?

O   my   Lord,   guide us   through   our   trou - bles
O   my   Lord,   my   Lord

fine

Till   we   rise   a - bove them   in   the   morn   -   ing.   2. Rise
3. When   the

Hymn: Irr., C. E. Couchman
Tune: AURORA, C. E. Couchman

D minor - 4 - DO

64   We Will Glorify

1. We will glo-ri-fy the King of kings; We will glo-ri-fy the Lamb;
2. Lord Je-ho-vah reigns in maj-es-ty; We will bow be-fore His throne;
3. He is Lord of heav-en, Lord of earth; He is Lord of all who live;
4. Hal-le-lu-jah to the King of kings; Hal-le-lu-jah to the Lamb;

We will glo-ri-fy the Lord of lords, Who is the great I AM.
We will wor-ship Him in right-eous-ness; We will wor-ship Him a-lone.
He is Lord a-bove the u-ni-verse; All praise to Him we give.
Hal-le-lu-jah to the Lord of lords, Who is the great I AM.

Hymn: Irr., Twila Paris
Tune: Twila Paris
© 1992 Singspiration Music/ASCAP

E - 3 - MI

65   Be Holy, for I Am Holy

PRELUDE

The Ho-ly One has called us, "Be ho-ly.

Be ho-ly, for I am ho-ly."

1. We walk in fear up-on the earth, Re-deemed with gold nor sil-ver
2. A roy-al priest-hood, cho-sen race, We are Your ho-ly na-tion,
3. We come to You as liv-ing stones, Built up and fit to-geth-er.

But with the pre-cious blood of Christ, Thro' Whom we are be-liev - ers.
No long - er stran-gers in Your sight But heirs of Your sal-va - tion.
Come fill Your ho-ly house, O God; A-bide with-in for-ev - er.

CODA

The Ho - ly One has called us, "Be ho-ly.

Be ho - ly, for I am ho - ly.

rit.

Be ho - ly, for I am ho - ly."

Hymn: 8.7.8.7. with prelude and coda, C. E. Couchman
Tune: C. E. Couchman
© 2002 C. E. Couchman

E♭ - 3/4 - DO

66 Our Fellowship

1. O Fa-ther, watch-ing o-ver me, And lead-ing me through life,
So man-y times I call to Thee In sor-row, guilt and strife.
And faith-ful, Lord, art Thou near-by To an-swer eve-ry prayer.
Pro-tect me, Lord, lest I de-ny Our fel-low-ship, Thy care.

2. O Fa-ther, Thou spared not Thy Son, But bought us with His blood;
From man-y na-tions, made Thou one U-nit-ed broth-er-hood.
Wher-e'er we gath-er in His name, A com-mon love we share,
At home, in dis-tant land, the same Com-mun-ion eve-ry-where!

3. Past chil-dren of Thy cov-e-nant, From eve-ry age and land,
As-cend-ed through the fir-ma-ment, And joined a might-y band.
One day, we hope to sing with them Thy hymn com-posed be-yond,
And with Thy con-gre-ga-tion form An ev-er-last-ing bond.

Hymn: CMD, C. A. R.
Tune: KOINONIA, Kelly R. Hersey and R. J. Stevens
© 1992 Pauline Stevens

E - 4 - DO

The Shining Shore

Hymn: 8.7.8.7. with chorus, David Nelson
Tune: SHINING CITY, George F. Root; arr. alt. C. A. R.

G - 3 - SOL

1. My days are glid-ing swift-ly by, And I, a pil-grim strang-er,
2. Our ab-sent king the watch-word gave, "Let eve-ry lamp be burn-ing."
3. Should com-ing days be dark and cold, We will not yield to sor-row,
4. Let storms of woe in whirl-winds rise, Each cord on earth to sev-er.

Would not de-tain them as they fly— Those hours of toil and dan-ger.
We look a-far, a-cross the wave, Our dis-tant home dis-cern-ing.
For hope will sing with cour-age bold, "There's glo-ry on the mor-row."
There, bright and joy-ous in the skies, There is our home for-ev-er.

CHORUS

For now we stand on Jor-dan's strand, Our friends are pass-ing o-ver;

And, just be-fore, the shin-ing shore We may al-most dis-cov-er.

68   When This Passing World Is Done

1. When this pass-ing world is done, When has sunk yon glar-ing sun,
   When I stand with Christ on high, Look-ing o'er life's his-to-ry,
   Then, Lord, shall I ful-ly know— Not till then— how much I owe.

2. Oft I walk be-neath the cloud, Dark as mid-night's gloom-y shroud;
   But when fear is at the height, Je-sus comes, and all is light;
   Bless-ed Je-sus! bid me show Doubt-ing saints how much I owe.

3. When I stand be-fore the throne, Dressed in beau-ty not my own,
   When I see Thee as Thou art, Love Thee with un-sin-ning heart,
   Then Lord, shall I ful-ly know— Not till then— how much I owe.

4. When the praise of heav'n I hear, Loud as thun-ders to the ear,
   Loud as man-y wa-ters' noise, Sweet as harp's me-lo-d'ous voice,
   Then, Lord, shall I ful-ly know— Not till then— how much I owe.

Hymn: 7.7.7.7.7.7., Robert M. McCheyne
Tune: Spanish Hymn; arr. Benjamin Carr

A♭ - 4 - DO

Triumphal Entrance

1. "Ho - san - na, King!" the crowd re-sounds; Their branch-es pave the dust - y ground.
2. "Our Lord! The King!" the host re-sounds; Their branch-es sweep the gold - en ground.
3. "Our King re - turns!" the trump re-sounds, And an - gel voic - es shake the ground.

mp   *cresc.*

Mes - si - ah wears no robe or crown, Yet all the mul - ti-tudes bow down.
Mes - si - ah claims His robe and crown; An - gel - ic mul - ti-tudes bow down.
The saints re - ceive their robes and crowns As at the throne all men bow down.

f

This Proph-et-King from Gal - i - lee Is on the road to Cal - va - ry.
This King_____ is
The ris - en Lamb in vic - to - ry Has con-quered death at Cal - va - ry.
The Lamb_____ has
The Son of God tri - um-phant-ly Will lead us home through Cal - va - ry.
The Son_____ will

Hymn: 8.8.8.8.8.8., S. J. Hardin
Tune: C. E. Couchman

Ab - 4 - SOL

70 Sing and Rejoice in the Savior's Birth

1. Glory! Glory! Sing alleluia! Sing glory to God.
2. Shepherds, do not fear. I bring glad tidings: A Savior is here.
3. Lowly manger bed, lowly the virgin who cradles His head.

Glory fills the earth; Angels rejoice in the Savior's birth.
Joy, joy for Christ the Lord! Jesus, Immanuel, the Son of God.
Hail! Hail, King of kings! Glory to God for the ransom He brings.

CHORUS

Have you heard? A child is born! Welcome, Star, that lights eternal morn.

a tempo

Glory sent to earth; Sing and rejoice in the Savior's birth.

CODA

Alleluia!

Hymn: Irr., C. E. Couchman
Tune: C. E. Couchman; arr. alt. R. J. Stevens
© 1987 C. E. Couchman

E♭ - 2 - DO

God Be with You Till We Meet Again

71

1. God be with you till we meet again! By His coun-sels guide, up-hold you,
2. God be with you till we meet again! 'Neath His wings se-cure-ly hide you,
3. God be with you till we meet again! When life's per-ils thick con-found you,
4. God be with you till we meet again! Keep love's ban-ner float-ing o'er you,

With His sheep se-cure-ly fold you; God be with you till we meet a-gain.
Dai-ly man-na still pro-vide you; God be with you till we meet a-gain.
Put His arms un-fail-ing 'round you; God be with you till we meet a-gain.
Smite death's threat-'ning wave be-fore you; God be with you till we meet a-gain.

CHORUS

Till we meet, till we meet, Till we meet at Je-sus' feet;
Till we meet, till we meet, till we meet, till we meet

Till we meet, till we meet, God be with you till we meet a-gain!
Till we meet, till we meet a-gain

Hymn: 9.8.8.9. with chorus, Jeremiah E. Rankin
Tune: William G. Tomer

Db - 4 - MI

Ancient Words

1. Ho - ly words long pre - served For our walk in this world;
2. Ho - ly words of our faith, Hand - ed down to this age,

They re - sound with God's own heart; O let the an - cient words im - part.
Came to us through sac - ri - fice; O heed the faith - ful words of Christ!

Words of life, words of hope Give us strength, help us cope;
Ho - ly words long pre - served For our walk in this world.

In this world, wher - e'er we roam, An - cient words will guide us home.
They re - sound with God's own heart; O let the an - cient words im - part.

CHORUS

An - cient words, ev - er true, Chang - ing me and chang - ing you.

We have come with o - pen hearts; O let the an - cient words im - part.

Hymn: Irr., Lynn DeShazo
Tune: Lynn DeShazo; arr. the ZOE Group
© 2001 Integrity's Hosanna! Music

F - 3 - SOL

O Come, Let Us Sing for Joy 73

O come

1. O come,   let us sing for joy, Let us   sing for joy to the Lord.
2. O come,   come be - fore Him now, With thanks- giv - ing come to the Lord.

1. Let   us sing for joy,   O   come_____
2. Come be - fore Him now,

O come,_____   O   come_____

O let us shout

Let us shout,   shout joy - ful - ly To the Rock of our sal - va- tion.
Let us shout,   shout joy - ful - ly To the Rock of our sal - va- tion.
Let us shout_____ joy - ful - ly

O let us shout

Hymn: 7.8.7.8., from Psalm 95:1-2; arr. C. E. Couchman
Tune: C. E. Couchman
© 1991 C. E. Couchman

E♭ - 4 - SOL

74   Abide with Me

1. A - bide with me; fast falls the e - ven - tide;
2. Swift to its close ebbs out life's lit - tle day;
3. Come not in ter - rors, as the King of kings,
4. I need Thy pres - ence eve - ry pass - ing hour.

The dark - ness deep - ens; Lord with me a - bide.
Earth's joys grow dim; its glo - ries pass a - way;
But kind and good, with heal - ing in Thy wings,
What but Thy grace can foil the tempt - er's pow'r?

When oth - er help - ers fail and com - forts flee,
Change and de - cay in all a - round I see;
Tears for all woes, a heart for eve - ry plea—
Who, like Thy - self, my guide and stay can be?

Help of the help - less, O a - bide with me.
O Thou Who chang - est not, a - bide with me.
Come, Friend of sin - ners, thus a - bide with me.
Through cloud and sun - shine, Lord, a - bide with me.

Hymn: 10.10.10.10., Henry F. Lyte
Tune: EVENTIDE, William H. Monk

E♭ - 4 - MI

5. I fear no foe with Thee at hand to bless;
   Ills have no weight, and tears no bitternes
   Where is death's sting? Where, grave, thy v
   I triumph still, if Thou abide with me.

6. Hold Thou Thy cross before my closing e
   Shine through the gloom and point me
   Heav'n's morning breaks, and earth's va
   In life, in death, O Lord, abide with m

O Father, Let Us See His Death   75

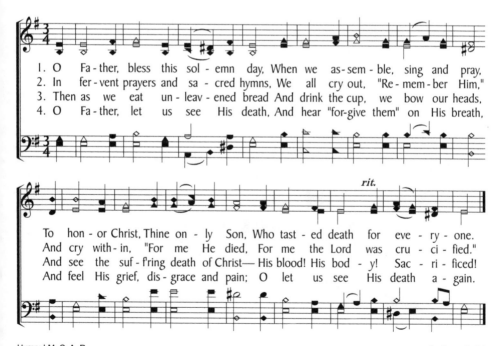

1. O   Fa-ther, bless this sol - emn day, When we   as-sem - ble, sing and pray,
2. In   fer-vent prayers and sa - cred hymns, We   all   cry out, "Re - mem-ber Him,"
3. Then as   we   eat   un - leav-ened bread And drink the cup,   we   bow our heads,
4. O   Fa-ther, let   us   see   His death, And hear "for-give them" on His breath,

To   hon - or Christ, Thine on - ly   Son, Who tast - ed death   for   eve - ry - one.
And cry with-in, "For   me   He died, For   me   the Lord   was   cru - ci - fied."
And see   the   suf-fring death of Christ— His blood! His bod - y!   Sac - ri - ficed!
And feel   His grief, dis - grace and pain;   O   let   us   see   His death   a - gain.

Hymn: LM, C. A. R.
Tune: R. J. Stevens
© 1994 Karl and Bonnie Hennecke

E minor - 3 - LA

Saints, Lift Your Voices
(On Wings of Flight)

ere is none like Him; None can com-pare; No god His e-qual, No prince His heir!
Have you not known Him? Have you not heard? God is Cre-a-tor of all the earth.
. Some will grow wea-ry, Sin they'll pur-sue. Serv-ants of God, their pow'r He'll re-new.

Lift up your eyes and see His great might! Soar like an ea-gle on wings of flight!

CHORUS

Saints, lift your voic-es, though dark your days! Lift up your spir-its, sing out His praise!

Up-ward the call-ing, bright-er the light! Soar-ing like ea-gles on wings of flight!

Hymn: 9.9.9.9. with chorus, Donald M. Alexander
Tune: Donald M. Alexander; arr. alt. R. J. Stevens
© 1984 Donald M. Alexander

F - 3 - DO

Look, Ye Saints! The Sight Is Glorious

1. Look, ye saints! The sight is glo-rious: See the Man of Sor-rows now,
2. Crown the Sav-ior! An-gels, crown Him! Rich the tro-phies Je-sus brings.
3. Hark, those bursts of ac-cla-ma-tion! Hark, those loud tri-um-phant chords!

From the fight re-turned vic-to-rious; Eve-ry knee to Him shall bow;
In the seat of pow'r en-throne Him, While the vault of heav-en rings;
Je-sus takes the high-est sta-tion; O what joy the sight af-fords!

Crown Him, crown Him, Crown Him, crown Him! Crowns be-come the Vic-tor's brow!
Crown Him, crown Him, Crown Him, crown Him! Crown the Sav-ior King of kings!
Crown Him, crown Him, Crown Him, crown Him! King of kings and Lord of lords!

Hymn: 8.7.8.7.8.7., Thomas Kelly
Tune: REGENT SQUARE, Henry T. Smart; arr. alt. C. A. R.

B♭ - 4 - SOL

78

I Am the Way

1. "I am the Way."   "I am the Truth."   "I am the Life."   "I am the Light."
   John 14:6   John 14:6   John 14:6   John 8:12

2. "I am the Bread." "I am the Vine."   "I am the First." "I am the Last."
   John 6:48   John 15:1   Revelation 1:17   Revelation 1:17

"I am the Son."   "I am the Lord."   "I am the King."   "I am the Christ."
Luke 24:70   John 13:13   John 18:37   Mark 14:62

"Be-lieve in Me."   "Be not a-fraid."   "Come un-to Me."   "I am the Way."
John 14:1   Matthew 17:7   Matthew 11:28   John 14:6

Hymn: 4.4.4.4.D, arr. C. A. R.
Tune: C. A. R.
© 2004 Larry and Doris Bailey

A - 4 - DO

Hymn Summaries

A FORETASTE OF YOUR REST thanks God for the times of peace that appear in our lives. Those moments promise that God will be with us in tumultuous times and that He will give us final rest in Heaven. (Isa. 26:3; Heb. 4:7-10)

ABIDE WITH ME borrows language from Jesus' appearance on the road to Emmaus to appeal to Him for His presence in the worshiper's life. Life and its joys are transitory, but with the presence of Jesus, even death holds no terror for the believer. (Mal. 3:6, 4:2; Mt. 11:19; Lk. 24:29; Jn. 11:35; 1 Cor. 15:55, 57; Heb. 4:15-16; 1 Pet. 1:24; Rev. 19:11-16)

ALMIGHTY GOD BEYOND THE VEIL describes the symbolism of the veil—the barrier between man and God—throughout the Bible. Under the Old Law, only the high priest dared to pass through the veil, once a year. But Christ's death tore this barrier, and now all Christians may approach God. (Lev. 16; Lk. 23:44-46; Jn. 19:12-16; Heb. 6:19-20)

ANCIENT WORDS calls the worshiper to consider the "ancient words" contained in the Bible. The words of scripture were delivered to the Christian at great cost, and they will both benefit him in this life and lead him to heaven. (Jn. 6:68; Titus 1:9)

AWESOME GOD praises God for the greatness of His nature and of His lovingkindness. (Ps. 47:2; Dan. 2:20)

BE HOLY, FOR I AM HOLY is an affirmation of God's calling us to holiness: believers through the redeeming blood of Jesus; a royal priesthood, holy nation and heirs of His promise; and together a body, a temple wherein God dwells. (Eph. 2:19-22; 1 Pet. 1:14-21; 2:4, 9-10)

BE STILL AND KNOW cites two passages that call the worshiper to remember that God is in control and that He strengthens us to serve Him. (Ex. 15:26; Ps. 46:10)

BE STRONG AND COURAGEOUS uses God's dramatic address to Joshua to inspire Christians to conquer their holy land, heaven. This conquest is achieved through boldness, confidence in Jesus, and obedience to His law. (Josh. 1:1-9; 5:13-15)

COME SHARE THE LORD invites believers to partake of the Lord's Supper and looks forward to the day when we will be united with our Lord in heaven. (Mt. 6:12, 14; 26:26-29; Lk. 24:32, 35; Gal. 3:28; Heb. 3:6)

EVENSONG contrasts the fading light of the evening with the constant spiritual light provided by Jesus. Because his Shepherd is watching over him, the believer need not fear the darkness. Even death is not a fearful prospect because of God's promise that He will resurrect His beloved. (Ps. 90:3-6, 91:5, 121:4; Mt. 13:43; Jn. 10:11; 1 Cor. 15:41-43; Heb. 6:17-18, 13:5-6; 1 Pet. 1:24; 1 Jn. 2:8)

EXALTED is about the ways in which Christ was and is exalted, first, in the prophecies concerning Him and the glories of His birth, then in His ironic "lifting up" on the cross, and, finally, in the hearts of believers. (Isa. 52:13-15; Mt. 13:14-15; Lk. 1:68-75; Jn. 3:14-15; 19:1-5, 18-19; 1 Cor. 1:23-24)

FATHER, HELP US RAISE OUR CHILDREN contains four prayers common among parents. It begins with an opening prayer then requests God's assistance as the children are maturing. It closes with a prayer that parents and children may reunite in heaven. (Deut. 11:19; Prov. 22:6; Eph. 6:4)

FOR YOU HAVE PROMISED beseeches God's protection and comfort, as a child entreats a father. It expresses faith in God's promises and a promise to tell others about God. (Ps. 9:1, 11, 14; 61:8; 69:30; 71:14-15; 79:13; 2 Pet. 1:4)

GIVE THANKS TO THE LORD is one of Israel's most common outpourings of praise. It is a phrase repeated in battle, incorporated into dedication ceremonies, and sung regularly as part of the Great Hallel. (1 Chr. 16; 2 Chr. 5; 7; 20; Ps. 100; 106; 107; 118; 136; Jer. 33; NASB)

GLORY YET UNTOLD deals with future glory in heaven. This hymn describes God surrounded by angels who praise Him and anticipates the time when all saints will participate in heaven's grandeur. It then lauds the Son Who left heaven and returned, thereby lighting the way for others. Each verse concludes by asserting the permanence of His glory. (Ps. 24:7-10; Luke 2:32; Jn. 1:4-5, 9; Rev. 5:11-14)

GOD BE WITH YOU TILL WE MEET AGAIN is a blessing from Christian to Christian, expressing the wish that God will be present and active in their lives, regardless of what faces them. (Deut. 33:27; Ps. 91:4; Song 2:4; Jn. 10:16)

GOD OF PRAYER is a song to God the Father, asking Him to remain near as we seek Him in prayer. It expresses to Him how we enjoy this communion, beginning with the day He first found us and lasting until the end of this life. (Ps. 72:20; 145:18; Prov. 15:8; Isa. 55:6; Lk. 18:1; 19:10; Phil. 4:6; Col. 4:2; I Thes. 5:17; Heb. 4:16)

GUIDE ME, O THOU GREAT JEHOVAH compares the life of the Christian to the journey of the children of Israel from Egypt to Canaan. Just as they were protected by the hand of God, so are we sustained by the Almighty and hopeful of being brought to the Promised Land. (Ex. 13:21-22; 16:4; 17:5-6; Deut. 5:15; Josh. 3:14-16; Ps. 28:7; Isa. 4:4-5; Jn. 4:13-14; 7:35, 41; I Cor. 10:1-4; I Jn. 4:18)

HEAR ME WHEN I CALL entreats God to listen to the prayers of the Christian, particularly in times of sorrow and temptation. (Ps. 4:1; 61:1; Eph. 1:23)

HE'S RISEN! expresses that, for the believer, each first day of the week is as bright with hope as the morning of the resurrection of Jesus Christ. It also links that sunrise to the way the darkness of death in our lives will be banished by our risen Lord. (Mt. 27:66; Lk. 24:1-6; Jn. 20:6-8, 18; 2 Pet. 1:19)

HIDE ME, O MY SAVIOR, HIDE ME asks for Jesus' presence and care. This song employs a figure from the Psalms—God protecting His people by hiding them from trouble. (Ps. 17:8; 27:5-8; 143:9)

HOSANNA echoes the words of those present at Christ's triumphal entry into Jerusalem, expressing the praise we wish to devote to God. (Mt. 21:9)

HOW LONG TILL THE MORNING? compares the Christian life to a night of struggle and turmoil to be rewarded by the return of Christ "in the morning." (Ps. 30:5; Jer. 49:14; Lam. 3:23; I Thes. 4:16-17; Rev. 6:10)

I AM THE WAY uses literal and paraphrased quotes of Jesus. In these quotes, Jesus claims to be everything relevant, prophetic, and magnificent. The ap-

plication is clear, comforting, and loving—"Come to Me." (Mt. 11:28; 17:7; Mk. 14:62; Lk. 22:70; Jn. 6:48; 8:12; 13:13; 14:1, 6, 15; 18:37; Rev. 1:7)

I SING THE MIGHTY POWER OF GOD declares God's power, wisdom, and goodness displayed in His creation. The intricate workings of nature demonstrate that God is still in control and present with His people. (Gen. 1:1-31; Ps. 65:6-7, 9-13; 136:8-9; Jer. 31:35; 51:15-16)

I STAND IN AWE exults in the greatness of God and the incomprehensibility of His nature. (Ps. 33:8; 139:6, 14; Isa. 4:2; Rom. 11:33; Eph. 3:18-19)

I WILL CALL UPON THE LORD quotes David's hymn of praise upon the occasion of his deliverance from Saul. (Ps. 18:3, 46)

I WILL WAKE THE DAWN WITH PRAISES borrows exuberant language from the Psalms to praise the Creator. Just as the dawn, the sunset, and the starry night praise God, so too the worshiper is overcome with the desire to glorify Him and encourage others to do the same. (Ps. 19:1-6; 108:1-2)

IMMANUEL, GOD WITH US highlights some of the paradoxes that marked Jesus' birth: the eternal God made mortal, the King of the universe dwelling in a borrowed stable, and the Creator of everything seeking comfort from His mother. (Mt. 1:22-23; Lk. 2:5-15; Jn. 1:14; 4:13-14; Heb. 1:2)

IN CHRIST ALONE sets forth the wonderful attributes of Christ and, from those attributes, expresses the confidence that the Christian may rightly have in Him. (Ex. 15:2; Song 6:3; Isa. 25:4, 53:6; Lk. 22:53; Jn. 1:9, 11, 14, 8:12, 10:28; Rom. 5:9; I Cor. 15:16; Eph. 2:20, 3:18-19; Col. 2:9, 3:11; Heb. 2:14-15; I Pet. 1:19; I Jn. 2:1)

IT IS TIME TO BUILD compares Christians to the Jews responsible for rebuilding the temple. The Israelites were lax in their work, so God sent Haggai to exhort them to diligence. Haggai spoke to them of a more glorious temple to come, the church. Employing many words and phrases from Haggai, this song reminds us to be diligent and joyful in building God's temple today. (Hag. 1:1-8; 2:1-9)

JESUS IS LORD uses biblical descriptions of Jesus to praise Him, then leads us to crown Him as our King because of the honors we have acknowledged. (Rom. 10:9; Rev. 5:12)

LAMB OF GOD outlines what it means that Christ is the Lamb—sent from heaven to be sacrificed on the cross for our sins. It then calls upon us to live such a sacrificial life that we too become lambs of God. (Ps. 23:4; Mt. 26:38-44; Jn. 19:21; Eph. 2:13; Phil. 2:7-8)

LET THE WHOLE CREATION CRY calls for praise to God from all sources. This hymn depicts all created things, all heavenly beings, and all people singing praise to the Lord. (Ps. 148:1-14; Rev. 19:1-6)

LET US KNOW JEHOVAH paraphrases Hosea 6:1-3 to emphasize the sinner's need to return to God and His abundant mercy. (Hos. 6:1-3)

LIVING WATER, BREAD OF LIFE thanks God for water and bread. Then, in contrast, it thanks God for the greater gift of spiritual nourishment through Christ, who is the Living Water and Bread of Life. (Ex. 16:14-15; Ps. 37:25-26; 65:9-13; 104:10-14; Isa. 55:10; Jn. 4:10-14; 6:27-58; 2 Cor. 9:10)

LOOK, YE SAINTS! THE SIGHT IS GLORIOUS portrays the triumphal return of Jesus to heaven after His victory over sin and death. Where once the "Man of Sorrows" was despised and rejected, now He has claimed the kingdom from the Father. (Isa. 53:3; Dan. 7:13-14; Acts 2:34-36; 1 Cor. 15:54; Phil. 2:10; Rev. 14:1-3, 19:16)

LORD, INCREASE MY FAITH comes from examples of faith in James' epistle and uses four similes in petitions for faith like Old Testament characters. Abraham, Rahab, Job, and Elijah exhibited sacrificial faith, working faith, patient faith, and praying faith. (Lk. 17:5; Jas. 2:20-26; 5:7-11, 16-18)

LOVED ONES is a series of requests for God's help when loved ones leave. It asks God for understanding when loved ones move away from home, for a reminder when they fall into sin, and for comfort when they pass away. (Ps. 119:169)

MAY THIS MY GLORY BE calls the worshiper's attention to the absurdity of being ashamed of Jesus when He is both glorious and essential to the salvation of mankind. It concludes by expressing the Christian's determination to "boast in the Lord."

(Mk. 8:38; Rom. 1:16; 1 Cor. 1:31; 2 Cor. 4:6; Heb. 1:6, 2:11; Rev. 21:23)

MY FAITH HAS FOUND A RESTING PLACE rejoices in our salvation. It emphasizes that our cleansing is not based on the teachings of man but upon Christ and the promise of His word. (Mt. 9:12; 11:28; Lk. 19:10; Acts 4:12; 1 Pet. 1:23)

MY FAITH, IT IS AN OAKEN STAFF illustrates the Christian's dependence on faith. As a staff, faith supports saints in their travel through this world, and as a sword, faith wards away error. (Eph. 6:11-17; Heb. 11:32-40)

NEARER, MY GOD, TO THEE compares Jacob's experience at Bethel to the reassurance we receive from God in times of trouble. It proclaims that God is with us even when we least expect it. (Gen. 28:10-19)

O COME, LET US SING FOR JOY quotes Psalm 95:1-2 as an invocation of worship. (Ps. 95:1-2)

O FATHER, LET US SEE HIS DEATH is a chronological review of Christians eating the Lord's Supper: they assemble, sing, pray, and partake. To assist in this feast, this hymn asks for God's help to envision Christ's suffering on the cross. (Lk. 23:34; 1 Cor. 11:24-26; Heb. 2:9)

O HOW GLORIOUS, FULL OF WONDER expresses wonder at God's creation. While exploring man's God-given role of dominion, the song reminds us of our constant need for Him, in spite of our lofty position. (Ps. 8:1-9)

O MAGNIFY MY MASTER expresses the Christian's desire to worship, evoking images of the great heights to which our praises soar, the greatness of the praise God receives from His people in both earth and heaven, and the greatness of the blessings that move us to praise. (Ps. 34:3)

O SONS AND DAUGHTERS, SING YOUR PRAISE celebrates Jesus' resurrection on the first day of the week and rehearses the events of that day. (Mt. 28:1-7; Mk. 16:1-7; Lk. 24:1-8, 36-40; Jn. 20:1, 19-29)

OPENING PRAYER is a call for unity and a prayer that as we come together, we focus solely on Christ, casting aside worldly cares and thoughts, recognizing that we have gathered in the presence of the Everlasting One whom we declare to be our Lord. (Isa. 44:6; Mt. 4:10; Jn. 1:1-5; Rom. 15:5-6; Col. 3:23-24; Rev. 22:13)

OUR FAITHFUL CARE takes thoughts from 2 Corinthians 1. Each verse glorifies God for the sufferings and trials He permits. The three verses, respectively, pray for the proper response to suffering, ask God to allow suffering in tolerable doses, and to expect more prayers as His children experience future trials. (1 Cor. 10:13; 2 Cor. 1:3-11)

OUR FATHER FOREVER praises God for His ability to guide the course of the natural world, hear the prayer of the righteous, and even wake the dead. It then assures us that He will use these abilities on our behalf because of the love He bears us as our Father. (1 Sam. 1:9-13, 20; Job 38:16-17, 31-33; Ps. 91:11, 95:5, 103:19, 139:13-15; Rom. 8:21, 26-27; 2 Cor. 5:8; 1 Thes. 4:14-16)

OUR FELLOWSHIP addresses the "joint participation" that saints have with God and one another. It also foresees "joint participation" in heaven. While it is a prayer hymn sung to the Father, "Our Fellowship" is also a teaching hymn rich in definitive language: "united," "common," "share," "communion," and "joined." (Ps. 143:1; Zech. 2:11; 1 Cor. 6:20; 1 Pet. 1:18-19; 1 Jn. 1:3)

PURIFY US calls upon God to cleanse His people. Only after He burns away the impurities that mar their character can they be suitable for honorable roles in His service. (Mal. 3:2-4; 2 Tim. 2:20-21)

SAINTS, LIFT YOUR VOICES (ON WINGS OF FLIGHT) draws on Isaiah 40, the "comfort" text for ancient Israel. It states the magnificence of Jehovah and His preeminence over all earthly authorities and powers, for God is Creator of all things. It encourages God's people to walk daily in His ways, even in difficult times; to lift up their eyes and see His greatness; and ultimately to soar to heights of joy and faith above the troubles of this world, as an eagle does on wings of flight. (Isa. 40)

SAVIOR AND FRIEND lists some of the many manifestations of the supremely sympathetic nature of Jesus. It concludes by appealing to the Lord Himself to love the worshiper forever (Mt. 11:28-30; Lk. 7:34; Heb. 10:23)

SERVANT SONG pleads with God to remake us in the image of both the Father and Christ, the great Servant. As part of this process, we ask God for humility and usefulness in His service. (Mt. 5:16; Lk. 22:24-27; Phil. 2:3-5; Col. 1:11)

SHALL WE GATHER AT THE RIVER? calls the worshiper to assemble at the river of life that flows through heaven. It further depicts the eternal bliss that God's people will enjoy once He calls them home. (Rev. 2:10; 7:9; 22:1-2)

SING AND REJOICE IN THE SAVIOR'S BIRTH celebrates Jesus' birth and portrays Him as God's glory and light on earth. It expresses the irony of God's plan, that a lowly child would become the King who paid the ransom for the souls of men. (Isa. 7:14; Mt. 20:28; Lk. 2:7-14, 28-32; Jn. 1:9-14; 1 Tim. 2:6; 2 Pet. 1:19; Rev. 17:14; 19:16; 22:16)

SOLILOQUY AND PRAYER quotes Jesus near the end of His earthly life. In these quotes, which are among His most moving, Jesus deals with the two most extreme phases of His destiny. In the first, He contemplates the inevitable hour of sacrifice; in the second, He prays to the Father for glorification after leaving this world. (Jn. 12:27; 17:1, 11, 13)

STEP BY STEP expresses a lifelong commitment to praise and follow God. (Isa. 25:1)

STILL THE CAUSE BEFORE US calls the Christian to stand and fight, not in a battle of flesh and blood, but in the war waged in the heavenlies. As we answer the call, we assume our place in the now 2000-year-old conflict. Like the early saints who first fought, we too are well equipped for this battle. We must not fear but look beyond the darkest threat and toward the bright victory of eternal life. (Mt. 16:24-25; Jn. 1:4: 2 Cor. 10:3-6; Rom. 8:31-39; Eph. 6:16-17; 1 Tim. 6:12-16; 2 Pet. 1:10; Rev. 19:11-21)

THE ARMY OF OUR LORD is a call to arms for complacent soldiers of Christ. It encourages them to join the fight and refers to those who fought bravely in the past—Christ the comander, His foot soldiers, their leaders, and fellow martyrs. The central message is that those who fight will conquer death and glorify Christ. (Eph. 6:10-17; 2 Cor. 10:3-5)

THE BATTLE BELONGS TO THE LORD expresses the Christian's confidence that although it may appear that the forces of evil are winning, in the end, God and His people will triumph. (Deut. 27:3; 1 Sam. 17:47; Isa. 54:17; Lk. 21:28; Eph. 6:11; Col. 1:13; Rev. 5:12)

THE FEAST OF LOVE explores the implications of the Lord's Supper and the universal church. Because all Christians are one when they partake of the one bread, we share the Lord's Supper with Christians everywhere and from every time. (1 Cor. 10:15-17; Jude 12)

THE LORD IS MY LIGHT paraphrases select verses from Psalm 27. It affirms trust in the Lord as a source of strength, hope, and comfort, and submits to God's constant guidance and presence. (Ps. 27:1, 4, 7, 9, 11, 13-14)

THE ROCK OF MY HEART takes the words of Asaph in Psalm 73 to express the Christian's dependence on God and God's faithfulness, even when the Christian's faith begins to waver. (Ps. 73:2, 21-24, 25-28)

THE SHINING SHORE compares our passing from earth into heaven to Israel's crossing the Jordan into the Promised Land. The image is that we are on the shore across from our "Promised Land," heaven. As we stand before, but across from, heaven's "shining shore," we can glimpse it because of our lamps. In the words of the chorus, "the shining shore we may almost discover," we understand that "may" means "are allowed to," and "discover" means "uncover" (as in "dis-cover"). The idea is that we can envision heaven now, especially since friends have already gone there, and though time on earth seems to pass quickly, we do not wish to delay our "crossing." Furthermore, we recognize the value of sorrow here— that it prevents us from being enamored with this life and makes us eager for eternal rest with God. (Ps. 39:4-5; 103:1-16; Isa. 40:6-8; Lk. 12:35-40; Heb. 4:9-11; 11:13; Jas. 4:14)

THE SPACIOUS FIRMAMENT reviews how the existence and operation of the heavens broadcast God's divinity. Although silent, systematic celestial activity announces "His eternal power and Godhead." (Ps. 19:1-6; Rom. 1:20)

THEOPHANY (HIGH ABOVE THE SERAPHIM) is a vision of Christ, not as seen physically, but through scripture. Through word pictures in Old Testament

prophecy and Revelation, we visit the throne scene. Here we gaze upon the Lord God Almighty, Jesus Christ. Also here, we respond as did the ancient prophets who had the same encounter—we lose our strength, then fall down and worship Him. The hymn closes with an assurance of our resurrection. (Isa. 6:1-4; Dan. 7:9-27; Rom. 1:1-4; 1 Cor. 15:51-54; Heb. 1:8-13; Rev. 5:10-14; 7:9-12; 11:16-18; 14:3)

THY WORD employs language from the Psalms to thank God for His presence revealed in the Bible. (Ps. 119:105)

THY WORD IS A TREASURE is a testimony of trust and joy in the eternal and never-changing word of God. (Ps. 119)

TRIUMPHAL ENTRANCE depicts three "triumphal entrances" of Scripture: Christ's entry into Jerusalem, His subsequent entry into heaven, and our entrance into heaven in His footsteps. (Mt. 21:1-11; 1 Thes. 4:16-18; Rev. 2:10; 3:5; 7:9-17)

WE PRAISE THEE, O GOD, OUR REDEEMER directs praise to God as our Redeemer. It also blesses Him as Creator, Guide, and Helper. (Isa. 44:24; 47:4)

WE SHALL STAND BEFORE THE THRONE is a sobering reminder of inevitable judgment. It describes the chronological events that will occur at the end of the world, emphasizing individual accountability, punishment, and reward. (Mt. 7:23; 25:21, 23, 31-46; 2 Cor. 5:10; Rev. 15:2-4; 20:12)

WE WILL GLORIFY calls Christians to worship God because of His greatness and His dominion. (Ps. 96:8-10; Jn. 1:29; 9:58; Rev. 19:16)

WHEN I CAN READ MY TITLE CLEAR pictures a time when the faithful will inhabit the heavenly dwelling Jesus has gone to prepare. In a sense, the Christian's "title" to the heavenly home is already "clear"—paid in full by Christ's perfect sacrifice. Still, that "title" may be encumbered again by the debt of unforgiven sins, and can be cleared of such only by penitent, faithful obedience. While clear title will be received, in fact, only in eternity, the hope and assurance of heaven provides stimulation to overcome Satan's temptations, the ridicule of scoffers, and all worldly cares, thus entering into eternal rest with God and Christ. (Mt. 11:28-30; Mk. 4:7, 18-19; Jn. 14:1-6; Jn. 15:18-20; Acts 17:32-34; Eph. 6:10; Heb. 4:9-11; 1 Pet. 5:8-10; Rev. 14:13)

WHEN THIS PASSING WORLD IS DONE describes the Christian's reaction on the day of judgment. When he beholds the destruction of the world, the majesty of God on His throne, and hears the rejoicing of heaven, only then will he realize how much he owes God. (1 Cor. 13:8-12; 2 Cor. 5:10; Gal. 3:27; Eph. 2:5-6; 1 Jn. 3:2; Rev. 14:1-2)

YOU ARE MY STRENGTH simply lists from various passages some of the things the Lord is to His people. (Ex. 15:2; Ps. 18:2; 27:1; 33:20; 40:17; 48:14; 71:5; 78:35; Isa. 9:6-7; Rom. 15:13)

Suggested Arrangements (†)

Certain hymns in this publication have a dagger (†) symbol in the footnote, indicating an optional arrangement. These arrangements have been employed in some congregations and been found to increase the effectiveness of a hymn.

25 Savior and Friend
       Vs. 1—soprano and alto
       Vs. 2—soprano, alto, and tenor
       Vs. 3—all parts

51 Nearer, My God, to Thee
       Sing vs. 1
       Read Gen. 28:10-15
       Sing vv. 2 and 3
       Read Gen. 28:16-22
       Sing vv. 4 and 6 (omit vs. 5)

Metrical Index of Hymns and Tunes

Index of Titles and First Lines